HARDPRESS.NET
HOME OF HARD-TO-FIND BOOKS

Peregrine Bunce
by Theodore Edward Hook

Address:
HardPress
8345 NW 66TH ST #2561
MIAMI FL 33166-2626
USA
Email: info@hardpress.net

PEREGRINE BUNCE;

OR,

SETTLED AT LAST.

A NOVEL

BY THEODORE E. HOOK, ESQ.

AUTHOR OF

"SAYINGS AND DOINGS," "JACK BRAG,"
"THE PARSON'S DAUGHTER," &c.

IN THREE VOLUMES.

VOL. II.

LONDON:
RICHARD BENTLEY, NEW BURLINGTON STREET.

1842.

PEREGRINE BUNCE;

OR,

SETTLED AT LAST.

CHAPTER XI.

WHEN Uncle Noll's letter reached the Tavistock Hotel, that worthy wight was " not at home." It seems that when he visited the metropolis, he was in the habit of varying the ordinary routine of his life, by dividing his time between his club; the theatre, of which he was exceedingly fond ; the social dinners of any of his remaining old friends, who were pleased to invite him ; and a sort of suburban semi-rurality ; a retreat in which he was wont to pass one or two days in every week, but where located not even his own confidential man

VOL. II.   B

knew.   It was generally understood that some
old school-fellow, retired from the world, perhaps in no prosperous circumstances, claimed
this attention, which Oliver Bunce paid him
without subjecting him to the remarks of others
of his contemporaries.   Some of the servants,
who were aware of the proceeding, went so far
as to say that it was his brother, who in early
life had committed some excesses which had
driven him from society, and who had long
been reported dead ; whom he visited ; but it
was generally believed, that whether friend or
relative, the object of his solicitude must be a
priest, or person exceedingly pious ; inasmuch
as Oliver, who never missed church twice a day
when at home, or the evening lecture when
there was one, invariably passed the Saturday
and Sunday with his friend out of town.

It may seem strange, as no doubt his faithful servant Limpus—(who, bearing the same
Christian name as himself—Oliver—he always
called, " O. Limpus hight,")—had taken all

imaginable pains to discover the " shady blest retreat," whither his master so regularly and periodically retired, that he had not succeeded in making the discovery. Noll, the master, however, had evidently some strong reason for baffling the attempts of the inquisitive. His mode of departing upon these hebdomadal excursions, was, like most other acts of life, eccentric; his portable wardrobe, upon these occasions, consisted of one shirt, one night-cap, and a minute leathern case, containing a strop, razor, shaving-brush, and tooth-brush ; and these, so collected together, were deposited in one of his coat-pockets. Provided with this store, and armed with an umbrella, he would walk down to the shore of the river Thames at Hungerford Market, call a waterman, and tell him to pull up the river.

Having given thése orders — wholly inconsequential to listeners, (if there had been any,) away he went, keeping as good a look-out a-stern as ever fresh-water sailor did, in order

to assure himself that he was not " chased."
When he reached Chelsea or its vicinity, he
would order the man to pull ashore. Sometimes
at the Old Swan ; at another time at the
Yorkshire Grey ; but seldom twice at the same
place. And if he had by any accident gotten
hold for a second time of the same waterman,
he would order him to the Red House on the
opposite bank, where he " heard there was a
pigeon match to come off." Upon which occasion he would wait until he saw the slice of
melon, called a wherry, in which he had been
pulled up, well on its way back to Hungerford
before he stirred ; and then the chances were,
that he would walk along the Surrey bank all
along to Battersea, and cross the river by the
bridge.

It so happened that Peregrine was wholly
ignorant of these strange proceedings, a knowledge of which would have imbued him with
some apprehension, that the object of his uncle's
attentive respect and veneration might some-

how interfere with his hopes and expectations
of provision ; but as Noll had pretty plainly
expressed himself upon the point, he might
have felt tolerably sure that nothing would
seriously mar his prospects if he behaved himself properly, as regarded his inheritance ; but
had he been aware of their mysterious dis-
appearance, his anxiety would have been much
greater than it ever was at not getting an
answer from the worthy old gentleman to his
invitation—no—he had written on the Friday.
Sunday came, and not a line.   The fact was,
Uncle Noll had boated away on Friday afternoon
—cold as it was—and there lay Peregrine's letter
at the Tavistock, unopened and unread.

Long before Sunday the whole affair between
Peregrine and the widow, and the offer and
acceptance, were notorious in the Hotel-Dumble-
dore ; and the lover and the lady were left to
themselves as much as possible ; " Mrs. D."
undertaking not only to soothe but amuse
Lucetta until the arrival of Miss Atkins ;

although the young lady seemed in a humour neither to be pleased nor tranquillized ; in fact, she had expressed a determination to Page, which, if carried out, would have made a nice bit of business of it ; but, short-sighted mortals that we are, Page little thought what was most likely to happen to *her*, when the governess really *did* make her appearance.

It was a great relief to Peregrine to have the *dénouement* of the affair known, so far as regarded the family circle, because he could now talk matters over with his invincible host, and open his heart to him upon points which he could not venture to touch upon in conversation with his intended ; and communicate to *him* in confidence, certain matters upon which they had previously communed together.

" I am sorry," said Peregrine, after dinner on the Sunday, " that I did not get an answer from my uncle.   I hate uncertainty."

" Everything is uncertain in *this* world," said Dumbledore ; " but 1 think, considering the short space of time in which your negotiation has come off, (as the gamblers say,) *you* need not grumble."

"Come off," said Peregrine; "*you* talk of marriage and its contingencies, important as they are, in sporting language. I look at such matters more seriously."

"Sport—sporting matters," said Dumbledore.—"No, no, I am no sporting man—' Non ego *Mendoza*,' as Ovid says.—Don't fight; shoot, I can't—put my *negaturs* on, in the season—no go then. Cock fighting I can't bear; for, as I say with Persius, ' In *cocktum generosa pectus*,' —ha! ha! ha!—and when we have been boys they often have peck't us—ha! ha! ha!"

"——— I don't mean *that*," said Peregrine, trying to stop him. " I never accused you of ——— "

"——— And as for horse-racing," continued Dumbledore, "that's a matter of *course*, and *stakes* and *plates*."

"No—no—no," said Peregrine, in a louder

tone than usual, " you quite mistake me ; my thoughts run all upon my own peculiar position. I feel myself very strangely placed about Lucetta."

" Oh, as the old senator has it, ' quicquid in *Luce* est.' I'll talk about her—ha ! ha !"

" She is an extremely quick girl—intelligent, and even accomplished—superficially," said Peregrine.

" Oh, accomplished," said Dumbledore, " I believe you ; she got a prize for a water-colour drawing—done by her master, I presume,—from the Society of Arts two years ago."

" A prize ?" said Peregrine.

" Yes," said Dumbledore, "what Horace calls an ' *Argente Pallet.*'—Ha ! ha ! ha !"

" That, my dear friend, is not exactly my point," said the affianced Peregrine. " I am not thinking of her accomplishments so much as the precocity of her feelings, and—I may say,— passions. Within the last four-and-twenty hours, and since she has been aware of the relative position in which we are likely to stand, I have been very much stricken by her conduct ; and indeed, in conjunction with her maid Miss Page, I think—I don't know—but I am quite startled."

" Oh," said Dumbledore, " as to her forward-ness in the love-line — ha ! ha ! ha ! — don't trouble yourself about *that*. I dare say, young as she is, as Ovid has it, ' *Puppies* amat,'—ha ! ha ! ha !—What's that to *you ?*"

" Still," said Peregrine, " I do assure you it would be a very great comfort and support to me, in my present position, if my uncle were to come down. I have secured rooms for him at the inn, confident in his compliance with my request."

" I think, after being used to his own com-fortable house," said Dumbledore, " when he gets into a Brighton inn bed, you'll have him roaring out with Horace, ' Quid *Fleas*,'—ha ! ha ! ha !—come, drink your wine."

" Yes, but," said Peregrine, " if I could but

B 5

get you to be serious for five minutes, it would
be ———."

"——— serious," said Dumbledore, " ha ! ha !
ha ! That's what you always say—why should I
be serious ?—that's what I ask *you*, as I ask
myself.—' *Molly* meum,' as I call my Sally for
shortness, knows I never cry—I look after
the fun, and *she* after the money ; and as I
say, she is a good housewife ; and ' Honi
soit qui *Molly pense*,'—ha ! ha ! ha ! Let's
drink her health ; or no, stay, *you* shall do
that,—and I'll give you the widow—that's it
—only I needn't give her, for 'gad you have
taken her yourself—a true bill—no kind of
doubt—all settled—not a case ' quod exit in
hum,'—no—I wish you joy, old fellow, and
deuced glad you came down to us ;—here's Mrs.
Bunce, as is to be."

" My dear friend," said Peregrine, " you have
no idea of the state of nervousness in which you
keep me by speaking so loud, as I said the very
first day I was here ; the walls of these houses

are so thin, that every word you are now saying may be heard, not only up-stairs, but next door."

" What then?" said Dumbledore,—" never say anything I am ashamed of—besides, my next door neighbour is my old friend Dick Hill— so—as I say, my talk is ' Vox et præterea *nigh Hill,*'—ha! ha! ha!—not but Mr. Dick, as I was remarking yesterday, is getting old—eh? as the poet says, ' *Dick age,*'—ha! ha! ha!"

" Come, come, let us go to the ladies," said Peregrine, who found, as usual, that he could get nothing like common sense out of his friend's head.

" Up to the ladies," said Dumbledore, " to be sure—' Toute *sweet,*' as the French say of the sugar; only you would'nt be so ungallant as not to drink dear Mrs. D.—my old Sally."

" Certainly not," said Peregrine.

" What wine will you have as a top-up?" said Dumbledore.

" I'll take some sherry," said Peregrine.

" Do, do," said Dumbledore, " *I* shall drink

her in ' *my deary*,'—ha ! ha ! ha !—but as it *is* early, mightn't we just take a turn on the Esplanade—one cigar—eh ?"

" You devote yourself too much to that infernal smoking," said Peregrine.

" I don't confine myself to smoking," said Dumbledore ; " I know the wholesomeness of the weed—I take snuff—and, between you and me and the post, in the cold winter nights, chew—ha! ha ! ha !—' *quid* et *nose*,' as Horace says—ha ! ha ! ha !—however, perhaps you may like to fly to the regions above; so I'll postpone my fumigations till you go home, and will take my chance of the night to enjoy your society and my cigar together in the open air."

It may seem extraordinary to some people, that a man having achieved what was the then great object of his life, under the most agreeable and prosperous circumstances, should, as soon as he found himself secure, and it may be called triumphantly secure, feel infinitely more unhappy than he had been during the period of his uncertainty ; but so assuredly felt our friend Peregrine. He had won the heart and hand, (soon to follow) of the very person of all others, whose hand and heart he was most anxious to win— the prize was his own, and he was the accepted husband of the handsome widow. But, to his surprise, it was only when he had thus carried his point, that his difficulties seemed to him to begin : all the technicalities of law details were, perhaps, trifles ; for, in his avowed, or rather self-admitted, and uncle-supported, character of fortune-hunter, he had settled himself at last ; but then Lucetta, and all the friends of her father, were to be conciliated ; and then the fear that all the surviving brothers and sisters of Mrs. Mimminy were to be known—and all *their* wives and husbands—and all their children—and all the uncles and aunts of the wives and husbands, and all *their* sons and daughters—and all *their* cousins and nephews, and nieces, and cousins-german — and all *their* great uncles and half-sisters, and half-brothers, and so on, *ad in-*

finitum: and of course, every one of these people had histories belonging to them; and as it appeared that Mrs. Mimminy had married her dear old Billy for his money, the chances were, that all the rest of the tribe were less profitably though perhaps more suitably settled, and that, therefore, Peregrine would be, in uniting himself to this charming creature, marrying *financially* fifty or sixty persons, as yet entirely unknown to him; but who, as in a thousand similar cases, having, like a swarm of bees, an established hive to receive them, are, bee-like, extremely apt to sting, if they cannot procure as much honey as they happen to want from the "stock."

Then Lucetta worried him sadly. Mrs. Mimminy, having secured him, admitted the venial deception she had played off as to the girl's age; and although the maternal misrepresentation had obtained him one chaste salute at the outset of their acquaintance, the disclosure of the truth awakened a feeling of something ex-

ceedingly unlike satisfaction in his mind;—in
two years he might have offered himself to
Lucetta, without, as he thought, any serious
chance of refusal;—and here he was, plighted
to her mother with only a life-interest in a
part of the girl's future certain fortune—and
then such a girl—so pretty—so clever—and so
much prettier, and grown so much more clever
in his eyes and estimation during the progress
of their acquaintance.

As has been before noticed, Mrs. Dumbledore
undertook to take "dear" Lucetta about with
her, not more with a view of keeping her away
from the "loving couple," than to separate her
from Page; for Mrs. Dumbledore, who held
gentle converse occasionally with her own maid,
had heard something of the notions of Miss
Lucetta, as to what *she* should do, if her mother
really *did* marry Mr. Bunce; so that during
the Sunday, except at church and at dinner, the
young beauty, as Peregrine, the moment he was
secure of the elder one, thought her, had not

any frequent opportunities of conversation with her intended father-in-law.

The next day — Monday — would settle the matter ; and even if Page were not so promptly removed, the superior influence of Miss Atkins, of whom Lucetta, with all her vivacity, and the provocation she fancied she had received, could not make a dear friend and intimate *confidante*, in less than a fortnight, would set all things to rights ; because, by Lady Dulcibella Damtuff's account of her, Miss Atkins was something unparalleled and unequalled in the history of first-rate governesses.

How matters mend—not when they are at the worst—but when one thinks they are going the way which a man wishes them to go ! Peregrine, whose nervousness, much like that of all braggarts, whether in love or war, increased as time wore on, and who really *had* worried himself into a state of excitement, which he in vain endeavoured to conceal from his gentle widow and bride elect, was all at once cheered, charmed, astonished, and delighted, by the unexpected appearance of Uncle Noll, who, on returning to London from his weekly task of pious duty, found Peregrine's letter in the morning, and forthwith ordered a pair of horses to his carriage, in which he had originally travelled to town, and hurrying Limpus in packing up, started from the Tavistock (which the said Limpus invariably called The Cabbage-stalk) Hotel in Covent Garden, and reached the Old Ship, at Brighton, just as his hopeful nephew had finished dressing for dinner.

The music of the spheres could not have been more harmonious to the ears of Peregrine, than the well-known sound of Uncle Noll's voice, inquiring after his nephew—it was everything to him—support, consolation, comfort. His presence in the family circle would give him confidence and respectability, and moreover his advice in mere worldly matters would be invaluable, when the time came for the trustees, and the brothers and sisters, and all the ark-like community of the relations of his intended, to make their appearance. Not a moment did he lose in hurrying down stairs to welcome his kind relation ; and although there was no sitting room actually prepared for him, he secured him one all ready to his hand, in which a cheerful fire crackled his welcome.

" Well, Peregrine," said Noll,—" didn't expect me,. I suppose—could not write—so I came —glad of your news—wish you joy—small glass of brandy, just to drive out the cold—and then —hey ?—where does your friend live ?—when does he dine ?"

" I will escort you, my dear Sir," said Peregrine,—" and you have no great deal of time to lose ; however, of this I am quite sure, you need not stand upon the ceremony of dressing —the lateness of your arrival is quite sufficient apology."

" I should think so," said Noll,—" if your friend won't take a man in boots at dinner in a November night, he won't do for *me*. I shall just refresh myself—a wash and a change—eh?—well, but, I say, Perry, shut the door—there you Limpus, mind—wait—tell them to show you my bed-room, and I'll ring when I want you —take care there; a good fire there—go."— Limpus went. —— " And now —— I say, Perry, —are you all fast—safe—sure, snug—no slipknots—no loop-holes—got *her* consent as well as your own?"

" As I told you in my letter, my dear uncle, so it is," said Peregrine, " I am a happy man— indeed the agitation in which I have lived since the termination of my doubts and fears, has quite bewildered me."

" Gad, then," said Noll, " as the old joke goes, you are two men—a man beside yourself —but why flurry and worry? if you've hooked your fish—bagged your bird—there's an end of all doubt. I say—is she prettier than Margy —wittier than Dory?"

" If you love me, my dear uncle," said Peregrine, " do not recall those names to my mind;

and above all, do not, in any fit of raillery
against me, glance at the sequel of Twigglesford,
at Dumbledore's."

" Hey," said Noll,—" what not the bugle
horn ?"

" Oh no, no."

" Nor the parson's pet ?"

" Nothing, my dear uncle, nothing," said
poor Peregrine, who, when restored by his
presence to a more perfect recollection of the
delight his eccentric uncle took in what *he*
called rowing him, began almost to repent
having sent for him. However, Peregrine was
right in his calculation; it was wise to bring the
old gentleman forward ; his wealth and position
in life would, as he foresaw, substantiate his
nephew's claims, and present to the friends and
relations of the widow a character to which
they could not object ; and more especially was
it important, as regarded the opinions of the
trustees ; for it had been made quite evident
to Peregrine during the last twenty-four hours,

that Lucetta was perfectly prepared to go any lengths to prevent her mother's marriage with *him*, and aided as she was by Page, he was not at all easy as to the probable success of her machinations.

Uncle Noll speedily despatched his preparations for starting ;—he had never before been at Brighton, and his ideas of its size and extent were consequently exceedingly erroneous ; and as for the technicalities of that town, he was in utter ignorance ; for when preparing for the march to Dumbledore's, a shower of rain suddenly falling, Peregrine told one of the waiters to go to the door and see if he could catch *a fly;* the old gentleman exclaimed, with mingled indignation and surprise, " Hey—what !— Perry, set a man to catch a fly in a November night !—and for what ?—hey—Perry, my boy, you *must* be very far gone."

" No, no, my dear uncle," said Peregrine, " not so bad as that—this is a way we *have* here." However, Noll seemed to feel rather uneasy; but his astonishment was run up to fever heat, when the man came in, to say that he was sure the Duke of Richmond, or the Marquis of Anglesea, would be back on the stand amost directly.

"Who, Sir?" said Uncle Noll to the waiter.

"They are the two blue flies, Sir," said the waiter.

"The Marquis—the what—the Duke"—stammered the old gentleman,—"two noblemen of such high rank, qualities, and character, to be called blue flies, by such a white-faced, whipper-snapper of a——I—hey—gad! I'll not stop in this house another minute!"

"My dear uncle," said Peregrine, "let me explain—so far from disrespect, the names of noblemen are now given to flies, as a tribute of applause and affection; and——"

"But what d'ye mean by flies?" said Noll.

Peregrine, assisted by the waiter, proceeded to enlighten the old gentleman upon this point, and, as luck would have it, their explanatory lecture was happily illustrated by the seasonable arrival at the door of one of the carriages in question.

" Hey, gad," said Noll, quite charmed when he was satisfied that no disrespect was intended to the aristocracy, " so that's a fly now — hey — why then, as the old joke goes, ' looking for a fly in Hyde Park,' is no such nonsense as it used to be — hey ? " and thus good humour having been restored, the affectionate pair were dragged with the wind right a-head to the scene of their future festivity.

It will not be worth while to recount all the details of presentation, introduction, hand-shaking, smile-exchanging, which took place upon the occasion. Suffice it to say, that Noll seemed to think that he ought to be privileged to give his future niece a chaste salute, but which, rather overpowered by her retiring timidity, he did not perpetrate ; but on turning round to Peregrine, he was heard by all the party to ejaculate, in what may be called

a stage whisper, " you are a lucky dog,
Perry."

Again was the family circle formed round the
dinner table, the procession to which, however,
was marshalled in a different manner than heretofore.   Noll took Mrs. Dumbledore, and Peregrine handed down the widow; Dumbledore
acting beau to Lucetta, who certainly was not
in one of her best humours; however, the ill
temper of one individual had but little chance
against the inveterate joyousness of Noll and
his host, who kept up a fire of words during the
repast.

Peregrine, who was most anxious to make
the certainty of his success evident to his uncle,
by the manner in which he conversed with the
widow, and the exhibition of certain little delicate attentions which he paid her during dinner,
her returns to, and acknowledgment of which,
could not fail to satisfy the old gentleman of
his nephew's security, could nevertheless scarcely
keep his eyes from gazing on the girl.   The

expression of her countenance was totally changed from that, which heretofore had characterized it, by, as it appeared to Peregrine, the feeling that she was an heiress, and that she ought not, with *her* fortune, to have been left under her mother's control as to *her* marrying, while her mother was at liberty to do exactly as she pleased ; but that expression was again varied by the anxiety with which she listened to the sound of the wheels of every carriage that passed the house. Miss Atkins was to arrive by one of the London coaches ; and although the Times had been suggested to her, she might have started by some earlier conveyance, and therefore might arrive sooner. Mrs. Dumbledore went on talking as usual, and somewhere about seven o'clock, the conversation having subsided into a lull, the ladies retired.

" I think, sir," said Oliver Bunce to Dumbledore, " if all I hear is true, and all I see I may believe, this gentleman, who honours me by calling me uncle, is not much to be pitied."

"I may say ditto to that," said Dumbledore; "and what's better still, the more you know of the lady, the more you'll like her."

"I assure you, Mr. Dumbledore," said Oliver, "I havn't been so happy for a long time as I am to-day. Peregrine's roving disposition will now be cured; for, as the old song goes—

'Here ev'ry flower's united.'"

"I am not conscious of roving," said Peregrine, mightily afraid of irritating the humourous raillery of his uncle, but at the same time anxious to repel the insinuations he had just ventured.

"Oh come, come," said Noll, "no tales out of school; but as I tell him, Mr. Dumbledore, marriáge will settle him—how old now, d'ye call the lady?"

"Delicate question," said Peregrine, "I have never ventured to inquire very minutely—thirty or so, perhaps."

"Thirty," said Dumbledore;—"'*Forty* si

necesse est,'——ha ! ha ! ha !——Split the difference——say five-and-thirty."

" The daughter is very pretty," said Oliver,
——" she seems fidgetty——eh ?——and restless."

" That," said Peregrine, " is merely an
anxiety to see the young lady to whose care she
is to be consigned this evening."

" Well, well," said Oliver, " settle it all your
own way ; and as far as I can contribute to the
arrangement and your comfort here, I am ready
for you ; you may say, Peregrine, of me, as
the old story goes, ' Nunky pays for me,' and
I'll drink a bumper of our worthy friend's
excellent port wine to your health and happiness."

Peregrine and Dumbledore, (especially the
former, as may naturally be believed,) were delighted with the warmth and cordiality of the
old gentleman, who, having drunk the toast,
declared that he would have no talking on
business till the next day, and, drawing his
chair close to the fire, continued enjoying him-

self until the usual summons arrived for the drawing-room.

" Perhaps," said Dumbledore, " if our new young lady is not over-fatigued with her journey, we shall have a little music to-night. I'm told she is a first-rate on the harp."

" So much the better," said Oliver, " more domestic harmony : come then, let us join the dear creatures above—we ought to have pity upon Peregrine—hey gad—come, my Benedick elect."

So playfully patting his dutiful nephew on the shoulder, the jovial old gentleman proceeded to mount the stairs, followed by his two companions, and the instant he saw the glance from Mrs. Mimminy's eye, with which his nephew was greeted, he gave one of the little grunts with which he was wont quaintly to express his satisfaction, and seated himself on the sofa next her, in order to improve his acquaintance with her.

This arrangement militated very seriously

against Dumbledore's design of improving the acquaintance of Uncle Noll, in whose joyous laugh and ready—apprehension perhaps is not the best word,—enjoyment of his "absurdities, this worthy blockhead felt infinite pleasure, and the delightful certainty that they should eventually become excellent friends. As it was, Dumbledore was obliged to content himself with announcing to Peregrine the arrival by the mail of some clothes from Nugee, with a " Hæ, *Nugee do send in maila*," and an observation upon, there having been a good deal of lightning, which, having been unaccompanied with thunder, he called the " *Dumb flammas Jovi.*"

Miss Lucetta, who had not yet made her appearance in the drawing-room, but who was no doubt in council with her " pretty Page," entered the circle, and communicated to her Ma, that it was quite time the Times should have reached Brighton, and inquired whether some servant ought not to be sent to Castle

Square, to ascertain the arrival of that coach; to which Mrs. Dumbledore gave a satisfactory answer, that the Times would bring any passenger to *their* door, which would save, at least, one and nine-pence in porterage and fly-hire.

Of course this financial explanation satisfied the young lady, who sat down at a table by herself, and turned over some prints and pamphlets which were lying upon it. Peregrine went over to her, and said something to her, of which she seemed to take no notice; and Mrs. Dumbledore was worried very much by noticing her manner towards him, because every body knows that hate grows like love, by juxta-position: and that these two people starting together in *their* relative situations in life, with disliking each other, or with a dislike on the one side, which was sure to engender a dislike on the other, was most disagreeable, if not dangerous. It, however, was in vain that Peregrine attempted to make himself agreeable. Lucetta was downright sulky, and carried her sulkiness to the extent of excessive ill-breeding ; for when she found her future father-in-law somewhat pertinacious, in his attempts to obtain an audience, she hastily shut up the book in which she pretended to be absorbed, and walked out of the room, to rejoin Page, and, in all probability, to inform her of Peregrine's insidious attempts at conciliation.

It was just at this moment that a rattling crashing of wheels, with a dead stop at the door, and a violent ringing at the house-bell, announced an arrival.

" Hey gad," said Noll, " somebody come— hey—that sounds like an omnibus."

" No, no," said Dumbledore, " ' *nemo mortalium omnibus*'—nobody comes here in an omnibus—no, no—this is the Times, no doubt— fast coach, and sure—' *tempus* fugit,'—ha ! ha ! ha ! Miss Atkins—here, Lucetta—where are are you ?"

Lucetta, actuated perhaps more by curiosity

than any other feeling at the moment, was too anxious to see Miss Atkins to require a second summons—down she came, differently indeed in manner from that in which she made her first descent to Peregrine, and close behind her, " paging her heels," Miss Page, whose desire to catch a glimpse of the new-comer, was nearly as strong as that of the young lady, but with perhaps more interested motives than those by which the said young lady was excited. Her hope was, that Miss Atkins would turn out a hideous skinny frump ; cold, cross, and ceremonious, rigidly frigid, and sourly sanctified ; so that the more than budding Lucetta would take a decided disgust to her, and throw herself into *her* arms as her supporter against oppression.

Page was just the person to wish this, and to do all that might result from the fulfilment of her wishes ; and had just got far enough into Lucetta's confidence to have almost made her hope that Miss Atkins might be odious, and disagreeable, so that she might thwart her, and take Page—one of the most artful, playful, and pretty things of her age and station—for her confidante, councillor, and future conspirator, against the governess.

It is odd enough, but certainly true, that to persons of strong feelings and sensitive minds, an arrival, let it be what it may, is always exciting; the present arrival was naturally more exciting than the ordinary approach of a governess would be, inasmuch as Mrs. Mimminy looked forward to *her* aid, as *the* support which she was to have against the *tracasseries* of Lucetta; and Peregrine was quite man of the world enough to know how very much would depend upon where the influence over the governess was to exist. Noll did not relish the disturbance, which, of course, caused the widow, the leading character in the drama, to leave his side, in order to receive the treasure which had been consigned to her by the Lady Dulcibella Damtuff. In fact, it was a break-in, and a break-

up; however, Mrs. Mimminy's anxiety to see
Miss Atkins was most natural, and so she
hurried out; and then came the thumping of
trunks in the passage of the house, and the
ordinary banging of doors, and all the gabbling
which necessarily takes place upon such an
occasion, and then Miss Atkins was graciously
received by Mrs. Mimminy; and then she was
ushered up-stairs to her room by Lucetta, who
appeared to like her more than Page seemed
to approve of ; and then she went and " took
off her things," (whatever that means,) and
then " would she have anything to eat and
drink ?" and the " no, she had dined at Craw-
ley ;" and then, " would she come into the
drawing-room ?—nobody but the family ;" and
then came the " Oh do, Miss Atkins," from
Lucetta; and so Mrs. Mimminy desired Lucetta,
when Miss Atkins chose, to bring her down and
present her.

And then Lucetta looked at Miss Atkins,
and, instead of a frump, she found *she was*

an exceedingly nice person. Mrs. Mimminy, at first sight, thought her rather *too* nice ; however, much to Page's dismay, it seemed quite clear, that Lucetta was very highly pleased with her ; and she looked so pretty, and the journey had flushed her ; and then she kissed Lucetta, just as if she had known her for a thousand years, and Lucetta said to herself, " I know I shall like *you*." And so she intreated her to come down to the drawing-room ; and in the midst of their intreaties, Mrs. Dumbledore came up, and *she* made friends with Miss Atkins, and was quite satisfied by the " things " she had on, after having taken her " things " off, that she was a very superior person ; and so *she* added her entreaties to Lucetta's, that she would join the party below, which she accordingly agreed to do ; Page looking at her, as she held a light to show the way, as if she could have poisoned her, conscious that the lady, who evidently was of her own school, but

in a much higher degree, would win the young
lady entirely to herself from *her*.

Just as they descended to the drawing-room,
onr worthy, impenetrable, and woolly-headed
Dumbledore was denouncing the Italian opera.

" Pay, Sir," said he to Noll, " pay for going
to the opera !—not I—if any lady lets me go to
her box—I go ; but to pay—no, no—hearing
it is enough, as our old friend Horace says,
' Audire est *operæ pretium* '—as for the pit—
gad—I'd as soon sit in a pig-stye—the ' Iter
pigrorum.'—Ha ! ha ! ha !"

At this juncture in walked Mrs. Mimminy,
Mrs. Dumbledore, Miss Lucetta, and Miss
Atkins.   Up started old Noll, whose gallantry
was as elastic at sixty-two, as it had been at
thirty. Dumbledore also was on his legs. Peregrine, who was standing still, looking over the
prints on the table, merely turned himself
round as the young lady entered the room—
their eyes met.

" Gracious heaven !" said Miss Atkins ;—
" Peregrine !"

" The devil !" cried Peregrine, " Kitty
Catheral ?"

" Yes—yes," said the governess,—" send for
a police-man—send for—Oh! Oh!"—And down
went Miss Atkins, Lady Dulcibella Damtuff's
accomplished governess, in a fit flat on the
floor.

" What's all this ?" said Noll.

" Why, Sir," said Dumbledore, " it is what
the French call a ' *Bully verseyment.*' "

" What does it mean ?" said Mrs. Mimminy.

" Ha ! ha ! ha !" said Lucetta.

" What are *you* laughing at ?" said Mrs.
Dumbledore ; " if there's anything wrong your
mother will have to pay the young person's fare
back to London."

" What is it all about ?" said Dumbledore—
" eh ?"

Hereabouts Mrs. Mimminy felt it due to her delicacy, to faint also; so down *she* went on the sofa — Dumbledore was about to attempt to relieve her, by throwing some water in her face.

" D." screamed Mrs. Dumbledore, " mind what you are about——damask sofa cover——water ——cost you five pounds, at least——here, give me a pen, I'll tickle her nose——mind, don't give me a new one."

" Ha! ha! ha!" again went Lucetta.

" Perry, Perry, Perry," said Noll,——" explain ——explain——what *is* all this?"

" I can explain nothing here, my dear uncle," said Peregrine, " this is most unexpected——I thought——but——never mind——we may set it all to rights in the morning——at present we had better go——yes, yes, I am quite serious——let the young person tell her own story — I am unequal to the task——I really am in a very unpleasant —— I cannot ——."

" Why, Perry," said Noll, " you—eh gad
—what, is this a true bill ?—what does it
mean ?"

" I will tell you all," said Peregrine, " but,
Mr. Dumbledore, I feel that I ought to
leave your house immediately—this lady—in
fact ——"

" Oh Mr. Bunce," said Lucetta, " what a man
you *are*"—and if anything could have com-
pleted the annihilation of our hero, it was the
triumphant look of the girl, who saw the consummation in one moment of all her objects—
his dismissal, and the rejection of the governess,
who, as the reader may more than suspect, had
been a *particularly* intimate friend of the flirt-
ing, flattering Peregrine, while bearing a name
which she had changed, in order to get rid of
the stigma under which she had laboured in
consequence of that very intimacy.

Never, to be sure, did bubble burst more
suddenly or unexpectedly, than this evening
party. Never did the members of any circle

find themselves so soon upset, separated, and half-killed: amongst the most turbulent and certainly most dissatisfied was old Oliver Bunce; because not only was he doubly interested, negatively and positively, by the position of his favourite nephew; but because he had been, to speak figuratively, almost dragged out of his bed, to hurry from the Tavistock Hotel in Covent Garden, to the Ship Inn at Brighton, in the county of Sussex, for no other purpose than to be a living witness of the disgrace of the said nephew—his consequent denunciation by Miss Katherine Atkins—and of the entire prostration of the scheme, enterprise, and undertaking, which the aforesaid Peregrine had, by his intelligence, talents, virtue, and accomplishments, just brought to its happy conclusion.

The scene was really lamentable—Mrs. Mimminy was carried to her room, exhibiting only consciousness sufficient to make the most furious resistance to any attempt of Peregrine to be civil. Miss Atkins, alias Catheral, was conveyed by one of the footmen, and Page, to *her* roost, sobbing and weeping most sadly; Mrs. Dumbledore superintending both *requiems*, so as to prevent any damage to the furniture. Dumbledore stood staring about him in dismay, unable even to joke, and Noll, at last, consenting to abdicate, in company with his discomfited relation, made active preparations for his departure.

After the sobbing had subsided, all was silence; but as Noll and Peregrine were descending the stairs, in a state scarcely to be described, Lucetta put her head over the ballusters, and said, in a voice which rang in Peregrine's ears most discordantly, " Good night, Mr. Bunce! —I suppose we shan't see you here to-morrow— ha! ha! ha!"

Dumbledore accompanied them to the hall, and—being really, with all his stupidity, a kindhearted man, having always liked Peregrine, and now liking the uncle—felt deeply about all that had happened; for although not very sharp, he was sufficiently alive to things in general, to conclude in his own mind that the screamings and exclamations, which had been so plentiful, must mean something too serious to be overlooked. However, they shook hands, and when they departed—the night was cold—the wind blew, and Noll did not at all relish facing the breeze—however, as the parting was unpremeditated, and the circumstances were strange, Dumbledore again bade adieu to his friends, so unexpectedly expelled; and upon Noll's observing that it was a bitter night, Dumbledore wound up his connexion with them with one of his worst jokes. " Yes," said he; " The air is a ' *nigger* and a *nipping*,' as Shakspeare says, —and as I said to one of my father's slaves, when I caught him cutting plantains in one of our plantations."

These, as far as the Bunces went, " were the last words of Dumbledore."

CHAPTER XII.

THERE is an old proverb, or saying, which, as indicative of a failure, pronounces that " all the fat is in the fire." In these days of delicate literature, it might perhaps be better and more suitably rendered, by saying that all the obesity of the animal has been subdued by the caloric ; but put it which way we please, there can be no doubt, let the real history of Kitty Catheral turn out how it may, that our hopeful Peregrine has been finally ejected from the Mimminy circle. Indeed, the following note, received in the morning from Dumbledore, seems to be decisive :—

" MY DEAR SIR,

  " It is extremely painful to write this
—but, after what happened last night, we cannot receive you here—nor your uncle Noll, as
you call him.—I liked him—to me he was a
regular ' *Nolli* me tangere' — I took to him
vastly, but the game is up ; my widow and
the governess have had their say out—*you* must
not show—Miss Atkins was bundled off by the
first coach this morning—so, hoping that you
and I may meet some time or another hereafter, I remain

      " Yours, obediently,
       " J. DUMBLEDORE.

" P.S.—We could not get rid of Miss Atkins
by any means till I had given her your address
in London. It seems to me that it is ' *re*dress'
she wants—she says she has been used very
ungenteelly — that she never could find you—
and that you know her attorney has got a writ

of *Fi-Fa* against you, if he could but find you.
—I said to Mrs. D., I was afraid it was a writ
of *Fie, Fie*.—Ha ! ha !—Adieu."

This missive of dismission was annihilation—
no doubt in the world remained, but that his old
friend Kitty, who he believed was settled with
a family in France, had betrayed all her own
secrets, in revenge for his conduct towards her.
They had been exceedingly intimate. Peregrine
had succeeded in rendering her what she too
truly was, by promising her marriage. He pro-
crastinated—delayed—demurred—suggested—
referred to his uncle's advanced age, his great
expectations, and so on, until at last he threw
off the mask, and admitted that he had no intention whatever of fulfilling his engagement.
They parted—and Katherine, who, with all a
woman's softness, loved him even for his faults,
would have been contented to take another
situation, and devote her talents to the assiduous
cultivation of the opening minds of her young

pupils, without marrying, if Peregrine's cruelty had ended there; but no—from the moment of their separation, he had never inquired after her, written to her, nor in the slightest degree interested himself about her; nor did he know that, from reasons important to herself, as regarded her own family and connexions, at least such of them as were aware of her indiscretion, she had changed her name, just about the time that Mr. Peregrine Bunce *happened* to change his residence, without leaving word with his landlord whither he was moving, or where he might be heard of.

What he had last heard was the truth. She had gone to France; and there, (having credentials from two or three families in which, until she unluckily met with our hero, she had been creditably and honourably exerting her faculties, and communicating her accomplishments,) her family advisers recommended — whether for their own sakes, or hers, we cannot pretend to determine — that she should assume another name, and the character of a young widow; for which they might perhaps have had some better reasons than at first strike one —and *so* she became Mrs. Atkins—" her husband, whom she had improvidently married, had been in the navy, and had fallen a victim at the early age of twenty-six, to the noxious climate of Sierra Leone." This was the history got up by the Catherals.

When she made an application to superintend the education of the amiable daughter of Lady Dulcibella Damtuff, her ladyship was quite charmed with her—her letters of recommendation were entirely satisfactory, and she entered upon the duty of idea-shooting under the most favourable circumstances, one condition only being made by Lady Dulcibella; that she should drop the *Mistress*, and consent to be called *Miss* Atkins. Her youthful appearance—her manners, &c. &c. &c. fully justified it, and her ladyship — why, perhaps her ladyship could scarcely tell — *would* have her to be *Miss* Atkins.

She had most successfully carried her young charge through a two years' course of education, until the young lady came with her mamma and governess to London, to be married to Monsieur Le Comte Henri Philogene Theodore Alfonse Chaumantelle ; when, of course, Miss Atkins was no longer wanted to teach the young lady anything, and accordingly answered Mrs. Mimminy's advertisement for a governess, which appeared in the Morning Post.

But now comes the black bit of this business, as regards Peregrine Bunce ; and which part, having told all else that *he* knew of the history of Kitty Catheral to Uncle Noll, he did *not* think it *proper* or prudent to mention.

The less one enters into particulars in such cases, the better for all parties ; but in writing history, we must not omit important facts, even if we feel that they ought to be touched delicately. During the blissful days of Peregrine's acquaintance with Katherine, sundry expenses had been incurred, for which he had unquestionably rendered himself responsible — if not legally, at least morally ; and so the poor girl understood, and so did the persons to whom she — for *his* sake — had become indebted. A surgeon and apothecary, a nurse, an upholsterer, a linen warehouseman, a wine-merchant, a butcher, a baker, a grocer, and lastly, an undertaker ; all had claims upon her. All these claims he had faithfully pledged himself to discharge ; but still she was the ostensible creditor, and when she talked of the writ of " Fi Fa," upon which the indomitable Dumbledore quibbled, she quoted, or rather misquoted, some announcement made to her by a low dirty attorney, to whom she had applied on her return to England, in order to relieve her from the difficulties and dangers to which, upon her arrival, she felt herself exposed. This course of proceeding many people may think resembles that, which the old proverb calls "jumping out of the fryingpan into the fire." Alas, Peregrine, with all his cunning, had so carefully contrived to manage his *affaire de cœur*, that no writ of Fi Fa, or Ca Sa, or any other writ, should ever touch *him* on account of poor Kitty Catheral.

It must be confessed that Dumbledore's announcement, of his having imparted to *Miss* Atkins *née* Catheral, the place of his residence, was to his selfish mind one of the greatest immediate evils. In all probability, a hundred and fifty or two hundred pounds would have settled all these demands, and the " gay deceiver" would, by paying them, have done something to modify his original criminality ; but no : his first determination on the subject was only strengthened by the frustration of his hopes of aggrandizement consequent upon the unexpected appearance of his once loved—or, at least once sought—victim ; and he resolved, that she should still be subject to all the ills and inconveniences of her embarrassments, in revenge for the mischief which she had done him in his last great enterprise.

With all his low cunning, with all his boasted knowledge of human nature, enlightened too as he must have been, as to the character of his uncle, by an almost constant residence with him, he did *not* know, and had not courage to try the experiment, that if, having told him as much of the history of his connexion with Kitty, as *he* in his worldly wisdom considered amply sufficient, had told him all,——the chances—— not to say the certainty—would have been, that Noll would have given him a check for the whole amount of the debts due. Peregrine had yet to learn the tenderness and susceptibility of his uncle's heart—of his devotion to the " fair sex," as the cocknies call women—and his inherent disposition to do good ; and even by an excess perhaps of benevolence, a stronger anxiety to do good, and be of service where misfortune unforeseen—innocence betrayed—or indiscretion repented of, were the causes of the calamity,

D 2

which his circumstances enabled him, when he thought proper, to succour and relieve.

But no—not a word of the young woman's pecuniary difficulties; a mention of those, Peregrine thought would touch the old gentleman's pocket; a detail of them would induce an explanation of their various characters and qualities; in fact, neither would he deprive himself of the money to save her, nor would he risk his uncle's good opinion by obtaining it from *him*; and in this mood he contented himself by urging the old gentleman to start for town immediately after the receipt of Dumbledore's letter; although Noll, who, as the reader already knows, had never been at Brighton before, was exceedingly anxious to see some of the humours of the place, and enjoy himself for a few days in a participation in the pleasures with which Peregrine and Dumbledore had assured him it abounded at that season of the year.

However, Peregrine, who certainly had—as indeed the old gentleman's visit to the coast

proved—a strong influence over his uncle, succeeded in persuading him to accede to his
wish of getting back to London as soon as possible ; and at all events, (if he could manage it)
before Kitty Catheral could have time to let
loose her six-and-eight-penny friend upon him,
at his then residence, whence his intention was
to decamp instantaneously without beat of
drum.

That Uncle Oliver was grievously annoyed,
not only by the defeat of his nephew which had
occurred, but by having been almost compul-
sorily made a witness of it, is not to be doubted ;
nor did the cold-blooded disingenuousness of
Peregrine, in misrepresenting the facts of the
case, tend to soothe him. All, however, that
he exhibited in the way of irritation, was his
expression of surprise that Perry, as he called
him, should not have trusted him with the whole
affair before ; just as if Perry—nice man—had
trusted him with half of it, *then*.

Upon poor Mrs. Mimminy, the explosion had

a very serious effect.   She liked Mr. Peregrine
Bunce ;——he, moreover, had made her believe
that he liked——nay, loved——her ; she had confided all her secrets to *him*——made his bosom
the depository of all her amiable weaknesses,
little suspecting the sort of man she had to deal
with ;——nor, to say truth of it, had it not been for
the influence of Mrs. Dumbledore, would it have
been at all impossible for her to have forgiven
the indiscretion of which he had been shown to
have been guilty in regard to Miss Atkins ; but
Mrs. Dumbledore's rigorous vigorous virtue
took such umbrage upon the occasion, that the
timid Mrs. Mimminy had not a word to say in
his defence ; nor had she nerve enough to stand
the increasing irony of Miss Lucetta, who
scarcely ceased laughing from the time she last
took leave of Peregrine till he and his uncle
had taken leave of Brighton, which they did at
about twelve o'clock on the Tuesday.

Now it so happened that Mr. Peregrine Bunce,
anxious as we know he was to shake off the

trammels of his London lodgings, had frequently promised some acquaintances of his, residing in the neighbourhood of London, and within some twelve or thirteen miles of that sink of sin and sea-coal, to pay them a visit ; and the present, in the fertility of his imaginative mind, he thought would be an exceedingly good opportunity to fulfil the engagement. He therefore determined, as soon as he had deposited his uncle at his hotel, to hurry to his lodgings, get his " things" packed up, place such trunks as he might not immediately want, in security, and start without delay to the neighbourhood of his friend's residence, the precise locality of which, prudential reasons, and perhaps an almost needless delicacy, induces the historian not to disclose.

To say that it was in Surrey is not to say much —nor much more, to add—that it was a fine looking house—stone-fronted, with pediment, columns, flights of steps leading to a sloping lawn, washed by a silver stream—or rather by a greenish pond, borrowed from the stream, and dammed up into a sort of little lake. Well trimmed plantations gave at once an air of security from the northern and eastern winds, and convinced the spectator that the master of the place had an eye to the " neat," as well as the " picturesque." Peacocks were to be seen perching on plaster ballustrades,—a boat was moored on the " canal," which was moreover illustrated by two swans, who, whenever any accident happened to the lock by which the majesty of the flood was maintained, went high-and-dry aground, and were forced to land themselves on the lawn for fear of swan-wreck.

The owner of this Paradise was the celebrated merchant, Mr. Joseph Nobbatop—head of the great firm of Nobbatop, Snaggs, and Widdlebury—a house famous all over the world for something which, to the uninitiated in mercantile matters, is wholly inexplicable. They dealt in everything, and seemed to deal in nothing —whether it were tallow, tea, treacle, tin, or turmerick—salt, silk, sugar, saffron, or saltpetre, nobody who visited Mr. Nobbatop's splendid mansion ever could ascertain. He was " a merchant," and there's an end : and what *can* be a higher or nobler character than a merchant of the first city in the world—and so we *will* call London, in spite of any charge of nationality,—particularly in business.

Mr. Nobbatop's turtle never tasted of tallow—Mr. Nobbatop's venison never smelt of saffron —neither were his *entrées* seasoned with saltpetre—nor did treacle interfere with the cookery of his second course. He was wealthy beyond calculation—his wife was agreeable, and in the way of family he had one son, and one niece, whom he had adopted as his daughter. Nobbatop, as to person, was in figure short, in face pale, his eyes quick and intelligent; but with all his benevolent disposition and admirable temper, his heart was not always in his own keeping—in company with his thoughts, it was eternally fixed and settled amongst his books in his counting-house ; and although whenever the conversation took a turn towards the subjects which he best understood, and in which he was the most interested, he became animated, and even eloquent, it was clear to those who knew him, that relaxation from his daily business did not afford his mind much relief.

In his ordinary intercourse with society, there was an evenness of manner which, with strangers, might pass for reserve ; but he was capable of noble actions, and performed them too, without appearing to sympathise with anybody on the face of the earth.   There was much beneath the surface ; and once accustomed to his apparently habitual coldness, he would be found—if he *did* take a liking—a firm and determined friend.

It will not require much trouble of the reader, in the way of divination, to guess the attraction held forth in the family circle to Mr. Peregrine Bunce, who, with his innate cunning, felt how advantageous it might be for him, while playing his game negatively against poor Kitty Catheral, by absenting himself from his lodgings, to be working actively in the hope of ingratiating himself with the exceedingly pretty Maria Grayson, who stood, in all but blood, in the relation of daughter to his worthy friend.

And here let it be understood why the thought should have so conveniently struck him ; and why, after having really made a very favourable impression upon Maria, whom he had met once or twice at parties and balls in the neighbourhood, he should till this juncture have abandoned all further pursuit of her. The reason was this : —he had always understood, and had perhaps formed an opinion of his own, upon his personal observations, that Stephen Nobbatop, the only son and heir of his father, was destined and intended to become the husband of his fair—or rather dark—cousin.

By a mere accident, a casual observation which he had heard dropped by some indifferent person, he discovered that young Mr. Nobbatop was actually engaged to another young lady, and that his marriage was to take

place in less than a month. This intelligence
not only decided the course he should pursue,
but the point upon which he would retire ; and
accordingly, although the season was far advanced, he proceeded to the Swan at Ditton,
which he proposed, at least for the present,
should be his head quarters.

To this humble, yet snug hostelry, he brought
his horses, and his servant——the break-up in
London rendering it absolutely necessary for
him to leave " no rack behind." Better accommodation for his nags he could have nowhere
found, than in the ten-stall stable of the said
Swan. Nor, if he had cared much about it,
could he have done better than he might do
there, in the way of living in a quiet way.

The associations past and present of that
sweet vicinage, are to those who know the *locale*,
delightful. There, embowered in peace and
happiness, lies, sheltered and dormant, only till
some new turn of affairs shall bring it into its
full blaze of splendour, talent of the highest

order. Look across to Hampton Court: what ·
recollections fill the mind—recollections *re*-col-
lected too, by one of its present worthy and ta-
lented inhabitants—think of the happy re-unions
which so often take place within those ancient
and time-honoured walls — breathe the purest
air of its noble walks—remark, too, the sparkling eyes, the ruby lips, and rosy cheeks, by
which they are adorned. Go to Molsey—(all
within a sort of magic circle of no great circum-
ference)—find there located, learning, intellect,
genius, accomplishment ; kindness unbounded,
and hospitality unlimited ;——turn to the un-
assuming Sunbury, in more than one house of
which the historian has been most happy—
return by Hampton itself, with its proverbial
sociality ; the place so justly favoured by a
lamented Monarch, who generously and nobly
proved when on the throne, the sincerity of the
friendship which he so cordially professed for its
inhabitants while only a private individual.

It is a delightful suburban retreat, and the

reminiscences of happy hours passed thereabouts, made Peregrine feel, not so deeply or sincerely, perhaps, as his historian, a charm and delight which it might seem invidious here to express in their highest degree.

In returning to this neighbourhood, as far as he is concerned, let it be understood, that if Hackney, Hammersmith, or Islington, had held in some of their mud-washed dens, Miss Maria Grayson, the calculating Peregrine would, with equal anxiety, avidity, and satisfaction, have taken up his abode at the Mermaid at the one, the Peacock at the other, or at the Pack-horse at the third. All *he* wanted to achieve, was the " *premier pas*,"—and therefore, although very late in the season, he affected barbel-fishing, and, under the command of the best of all piscators in those parts, Mr. William Rogerson, (worthy of commendation from Izaak Walton himself,) he betook himself to the afore-named Swan at Ditton.

It is somewhat remarkable, or perhaps one

might better say, strongly indicative of the self-ishness of Peregrine's character, that he had not one single individual friend of his own age or standing in life, in whom he reposed a confidence, nor indeed with whom he even corresponded. Everything centred in self; so that when he fancied he was triumphing, there was nobody to whom he could impart his success, and when, as in the present instance, he found himself defeated, he had not an associate to sympathise with him in his misfortunes.

Izaak Walton, and all his authorities and disciples, pronounce and proclaim the sport of the angle to be pre-eminently soothing, and even exhilarating.

> " O the gallant fisher's life,
>   Is the best of any ;
> 'Tis full of pleasure, free from strife,
>   And 'tis belov'd by many.
>   Other joys
>   Are but toys,
>   Only this
>   Lawful is,
>   For our skill
>   Breeds no ill,
>   But, content and pleasure."

So sings Piscator to Coridon, in the words
of Jo. Chalkhill. — Hear again the worthy
Cotton :—

> " The angler is free
>   From the cares that Degree
>   Finds itself with so often tormented ;
>   And although we should slay
>   Each a hundred a day,
>   'Tis a slaughter needs ne'er be repented.
>
> " We care not who says,
>   And intends to dispraise,
> That an angler to a fool is next neighbour,
>   Let him prate—what care we,
>   We're as honest as be,
> And let him take *that* for his labour."

This is gay, joyous, and for the most part a
true picture of that amusement in which some
exceedingly wise people find none. There is a
calm repose, mingled with a constant interest
in the sport, most soothing, and most delightful
to those who, worried by business, hurried by
engagements, are doomed to the noise and
bustle of great cities, and the senseless din of
what is called society. The quietude of the

beautiful stream—the freshness of the air—
the fragrance of the flowers—the music of the
birds—form a combination invaluable to him
whose head is over-worked, and whose heart is
not at ease. It yields a balm which those alone
who have tasted it, can appreciate.

> " Away then, away,
> We lose sport by delay,
> But first leave our sorrows behind us ;
> If Miss Fortune should come,
> We are all gone from home,
> And a fishing she never can find us."

However just this is, the reader must, by this
time, know enough of Mr. Peregrine Bunce, to
be quite sure that his object in transporting
himself to his present quarters, was not exactly
that which he professed it to be ; nor indeed
was November a season altogether calculated to
realize all the bright visions of the enthusiastic
angler.

As to the particular sport upon which—because he could ostensibly hit upon no other
—he had fixed, there does exist a difference of

opinion, and it seems but just and fair to set down what Sir John Hawkins has recorded of it.

Sir John says, " Fishing for barbel is at best but a dull recreation——they are a sullen fish, and bite but slowly. The angler drops in his bait——the bullet at the bottom of the line fixes it to one spot of the river. Tired with waiting for a bite he generally lays down his rod, and exercising the patience of a setting dog, waits till he sees the top of his rod move ; then begins a struggle between him and the fish, which *he* calls his sport, and that being over, he lands his prize, fresh baits his hook, and lays in for another."

But dull as Sir John seems to make out this what *we do* call sport, the anecdote which he gives immediately after the above passage, exhibits the feelings of an inveterate angler in a somewhat striking point of view.

" Living," says he, " some years ago in a village on the banks of the Thames, I was

used in the summer months to be much on
the river. It chanced, that at Shepperton,
where I had been for a few days, I frequently
passed an elderly gentleman in his boat, who
appeared to be fishing at different stations for
barbel. After a few salutations had passed
between us, and we had become a little acquainted, I took occasion to inquire what diver-
sion he had met with.

" ' Sir,' says he, ' I have had but bad luck
to-day, for I fish for barbel, which you know are
not to be caught like gudgeons.'

" ' It is very true,' answered I, ' but what
you want in tale I suppose you make up in
weight.'

" ' Why, Sir,' says he, ' that is just as it
happens ; it is true I like the sport, and love to
catch fish, but my great delight is *in going after
them*. I tell you what, Sir,' continued he, ' I
am a man in years, and have used the sea all
my life [he had been an India captain], but I
mean to go no more. I have bought that house

which you see there, (pointing to it,) for the sake of fishing.   I get into this boat (which he was then mopping) on a Monday morning, and fish on till Saturday night, for barbel, as I told you, for that is my delight ; and this I have done for a month together, and in all that while have not had one bite[1].' "

Before we quit this subject, as regards either sport generally, or barbelism particularly, let us just look at the remarks of the Editor upon the attested Calendar sent by the *Catcher* to Mr. Bartholomew Lowe, in Drury Lane, Feb. 24, 1766, in which he distinctly registers the fact, that "from the year 1753 to the year 1764, being the result of ten years, one month, and five days' angling, he had ' given to the public,' *i. e.* caught, forty-seven thousand one hundred and twenty fish."

Whereupon the Editor—and we give it as a set-off to the patient endurance of the maritime

[1] Sir J. Hawkins on Walton, pp. 290, 291.—Ed. 1815.

barbel-fisher at Shepperton—says, " If I had the honour of an acquaintance with this keen and laborious sportsman, I might possibly at times have checked him in the ardour of his pursuit, by reminding him of that excellent maxim, ' ne quid nimis,' *i. e.* nothing too much. The pleasure of angling consists not so much in the number of fish we catch, as in the exercise of our art, the gratification of our hopes, and the reward of our skill and ingenuity. Were it possible for an angler to be sure of every cast of his fly, so that for six hours his hook should never come home without a fish on it, angling would be no more a recreation than the sawing of stone, or the pumping of water."

This is perfectly true—the excitement depends upon the uncertainty. One word more as to barbel, and an end :—In the Quarterly Review, No. 133, under the head "*Angling,*" we are introduced to a certain Dame Juliana, (a sister, as supposed, of Richard Lord Berners, of Essex,) who became Prioress of Sopewell, in the year 1400, who spake thus of barbel, according to her commentator :—

" The barbylle is a sweete fysshe ; but it is a quasy mete, and a perylous, for mann'ys body. For comynly, he givyth an introduxion to the febres ; and yf he be eaten raw"—Hear it not Comus—" he may be cause of mann'ys deeth, wyche hath oft be seen."

Whereupon the said learned and accomplished reviewer, who knoweth well the angler's art, as well indeed as he knoweth more things than many other men, says—

" That raw barbel *ought* to cause the death of any civilized, unfeathered two-legged animal, all cooks will allow ; that such an event should have been frequent, can only be accounted for by the delightful state of unsophisticated nature, which prevailed in the fifteenth century."

Here then leave we Mr. Peregrine Bunce's *ostensible* piscatory pursuits. Knowing their particular object it may seem that too much time has been expended on the really scientific part of

the affair.   However, as it is not impossible
that Mr. Peregrine himself may be obliged to
answer certain questions at the house of his
opulent friend Mr. Nobbatop, when he arrives
there, touching his sport, perhaps no great harm
has been done by the digression.

CHAPTER XIII.

On the next, or rather first, Sunday, after Church, Mr. Peregrine Bunce began his course of amatory proceedings; and, aware that there was generally a little re-union at luncheon at Mr. Nobbatop's mansion, at that period of that day in each week, he proceeded on horseback, followed by his servant, to the gates, which he had but once before passed in his life, and that upon the occasion of inquiring after the ladies, whose carriage had met with some accident in returning from one of the parties at which he had had the pleasure of meeting them.

Then, Mr. Nobbatop had certainly given him an invitation to dinner, of which, for the reasons

of which we are aware, and in the belief that
Maria Grayson was the *fiancée* of Mr. Nobbatop, jun., he did not then think it worth while
to avail himself. His almost immediate departure from the neighbourhood prevented any
repetition of his call, or of his friend's bidding ;
however, the case being now altered, and Peregrine being, as usual, perfectly sure that his
person, manners, and conversation, had made a
favourable impression upon the young lady, he
ventured to build his hopes upon this slight
foundation, and endeavour to revive the acquaintance——for his own benefit.

To the servant's inquiry at the lodge, the
answer was, that Mr. Nobbatop *was* at home ;
and accordingly our aspiring hero proceeded
along the drive to the door of the mansion, which
closed as he first advanced, but was opened at
his nearer approach by some exceedingly smartly
liveried footmen, who, upon his dismounting,
conducted or rather ushered him to the dinner-

room, in which, as he fully anticipated, the luncheon had been spread.

The announcement of his name, it must be confessed, fell as far short of his own expectations of effect, as did our worthy Pepys' new periwig at church; inasmuch as Nobbatop himself, in the multiplicity of the avocations, in which he was perpetually involved, had entirely forgotten all about him. Not so, however, the ladies—especially Miss Grayson, who not only had *not* forgotten him, but really remembered him with pleasure. They were delighted to see him—how long had he been in their neighbourhood?—where was he staying?—what would he take? and so on; all of which questions convinced the master of the house that Peregrine *was* somebody whom *he* ought not to have forgotten, and therefore three or four *luncheonisers* were " pushed,"— not from their stools, but huddled up into a crush, to make room for the new comer, who, finding how graciously he was received by the fairer part of the creation, poked himself between Mrs. Nobbatop and Miss Grayson, apologizing with his " wonted grace," to a poor dear little girl, with plaited tails, who, in the concussion, was thrust out of the line of feeders, and forced to sit upon somebody's knee, to finish her repast with a raspberry puff.

The agreeableness of Mr. Peregrine Bunce's manner, the playfulness of his conversation, and the familiarity of his style, as regarded Mrs. Nobbatop and Miss Grayson, all conduced to convince Mr. Nobbatop that he had been guilty of some most serious violation of good manners, in forgetting not only the person, but even the name of a gentleman, with whom it was quite clear he ought to be remarkably intimate. Whereupon, he determined, that as soon as luncheon should break up, he would endeavour to make amends for his neglect, by inviting him to dinner, and cultivating an acquaintance which appeared so exceedingly agreeable to

E 2

his wife, and (as he called Maria Grayson) his daughter.

Can there be a doubt as to the reply to the invitation ? One of the vulgar errors which have obtained in society is, that a bishop, upon being elevated to his see, says, " Nolo Episcopari," when the dignity is offered to him. No such thing occurs—no such hypocritical refusal forms part of any of the ceremonies connected with his consecration, his homage, or his enthronement—but so goes the cockneyism. But even if such *were* the fact, in the case of Episcopacy, the example was not likely to be followed upon an occasion like the present by Peregrine, who, in declining the proffered dinner, might have, as he would himself have said, " thrown away a chance." Wherefore did he accept the said invitation, not a little elated at the manner in which he had been-welcomed by Maria Grayson, and rather sanguine as to results.

" We can, of course, give you a bed," said

Nobbatop—not at the moment able to recollect the name of his intimate friend.

" No, thank you," said Peregrine; " my headquarters are not far off,—and ———"

" But," said Mr. Nobbatop, " you had better sleep here—why not let your servant go back to your inn, bring your things to dress, and so stay with us to-morrow ?"

" My horses are here," said Peregrine, " and ——— "

" Let them stay here," said Nobbatop; " there's plenty of room for them—they won't be worse fed, or taken care of, here, than at your inn ; so just order your servant to direct them to be well housed—send back for your things, and make up your mind to be comfortable where you are—only being Sunday, I can't give you any fishing, and even if it were Monday, I doubt whether I could give you any very good sport."

Peregrine had fallen like a diamond into

cotton—this was beyond his hopes—and after a certain number of protestations and expressions of gratitude, and of fears of inconvenience, and all that sort of thing, he submitted to Mr. Nobbatop's directions, and, having summoned his servant, gave him his orders according to the suggestions of his excellent host.

While he was absent upon this mission, Mr. Nobbatop said to his wife—

" Charlotte, dear ! what is the gentleman's name that we are so very intimate with ? "

" Bunce," said Mrs. Nobbatop : " don't you recollect how agreeable he was at Lady Jane Ginger's ball last year ? and how very good-natured we found him after our accident at dear Mrs. Macsnigger's party, when the carriage got swamped in the river ? "

" Oh, ah ! " said Nobbatop ; " yes, I do remember,"—not that he did in the slightest degree,—" then I have done right in asking him to stop ? "

" Quite right," said Maria ; " for I think him
a most agreeable person, and flatter myself that
we are exceedingly lucky that his fishing propensities have brought him into our neighbourhood."

Fishing propensities, indeed !

He must be a very silly person who does not
very soon discover whether he is, or is not,
likely to be what is absurdly called " popular,"
with any body upon whom he has fixed his eye
or mind. Peregrine's vanity upon the present
occasion was not needed to assure him of the
character of his reception by Maria Grayson.
She really *had been* pleased with him, as many
a girl might have been ; and if he had not
laboured under the misapprehension about her
engagement to her cousin, he *then* might have
achieved his great object, and been settled ; for
there was no doubt as to her uncle's intentions
as regarded her. She was called, upon the
imaginary scale, to which we have before referred—a hundred thousand pounds fortune—

E 4

but, reducing it to reality, her uncle really *did* mean, that whenever she married with his consent——and she was not likely to marry without it——she should have forty thousand pounds down —supernaculum.

Maria Grayson had, for two or three years, been the hunted, of Hussars,——the persecuted, of Lancers,——the apple of contention between small town dandies, young officials, and sons of country gentlemen further down the road, who admired her, as she justly deserved to be admired, but who, (such is the gross unsentimentality of *La Jeune Angleterre*,) looked more to the worldly than spiritual feeling of love, and bowed before the beautiful picture, in hopes of its being sent home in a golden frame.

Maria Grayson was quite aware of all this— she was not to be dazzled by an embroidered jacket, nor tickled with a pair of black mustachios—she had taste, sense, and feeling ; and it did so happen, that Peregrine—luckiest of his sex—had interested her more than any man she

had yet seen — their acquaintance had been
slight, their association brief. He had been
deputed to take care of her at the party remembered by her mother, at Lady Jane Ginger's—
he had led her to supper, he had made himself
particularly agreeable, and had eventually handed
her to the carriage—and it so happened, that
then, labouring under the impression that she
was engaged, he was not acting a part; so
that the natural playfulness of his conversation
made, unconsciously to *him*, its effect, and as
we have heard the bright-eyed girl herself con-
fess, she was quite pleased to see him again
under their roof.

To please his wife, his son, and his adopted
daughter, was to please Mr. Nobbatop; he had
neither time nor inclination for discussions or
arguments at home—home was to him, as far as
it went, repose from worldly cares; and, perfectly satisfied with the security that all went
well *there*, afforded him by the exemplary characters of the members of his family, he cared

nothing for what happened, who were asked, who excluded, so as he saw smiles on the faces of those he loved, and a hearty welcome given to those who were beloved or beliked by them.

The junior Nobbatop was, upon the present occasion, absent—he was with his " ladie love," progressing, as the Americans say, to a happy conclusion with *his* suit ; at which Peregrine did by no means lament, inasmuch as his experience in the scrutinizing qualities of brothers and cousins did not at all increase his desire for any association with such relations or connexions during the process of heart-winning. Certainly, Peregrine never stood upon so firm a footing as this, since we have known him—a charming girl pre-possessed in his favour—the master of the house most friendly, and his wife exceedingly kind—this was evidently his time to make play—of that he was aware, and accordingly directed his servant to bring a *large* portmanteau and two *sacs de nuit*, and to tell the Swan, that he might probably not return for three or four days.

It may offend some readers to know, that Mr. Nobbatop's dinners—that is to say, meetings of friends at dinner—were regularly fixed for Sundays ; the true and just reason for that innovation, as some people call it, upon Christian —or rather protestant—propriety—being, that upon no day excepting the day of rest, set apart for abstinence from labour, could the indefatigable Nobbatop find time or opportunity to exhibit his hospitality or welcome his acquaintance. Whether this notion was really and truly less pious, or less virtuous, than in the times when the squire uniformly entertained the parson of his parish at dinner on the Sunday ; or whether all the Roman Catholics in the world are to be condemned for ever, for keeping Sunday as a holiday, after the holy part of the day is past, who shall say? but this we *will* say, that attempting to deprive the working classes of their air, their exercise, their amusements, and their

one day's hot dinner in the week, by a rigid
enforcement of puritanical regulations, which
would have disgraced the commonwealth, are at
once indicative of hypocrisy, tyranny, and cruelty, and exhibit a spirit excited by a desire to
drive those who are really inclined to religion,
into a reckless disregard of all its just laws and
ordinances. A poor man must not be shaved
on a Sunday morning, to go to church; his
wife must not send their dinner to be baked,
because it is wrong for bakers to work, while, if
she stays at home to cook it, she must abstain
from divine service herself. In the afternoon,
they must not indulge themselves with a cake
and a glass of ale, after a healthful walk with
their poor children. All public-houses are to
be closed; all merriment is to be stopped; and
the day set apart by the Divinity, as the day of
recreation, is to be made a day of gloom and
confinement for those who, as we have just
said, have but that one day in the week in which
they can enjoy air, exercise, the society of their

families, and the harmless amusements to which, in far better days than these, the much better English people were universally accustomed.

Nobbatop was as pious and as charitable a man as his neighbours—he was universally esteemed—he righteously fulfilled all the social duties of life ; but he did not see why he should not draw round him on the Sunday,—his only day of leisure—his nearest and dearest friends ; and enjoy, with proper gratitude, the good things of this world, which, under Providence, his own honest industry had earned ; and so Nobbatop always had a snug party on the Sunday, never once omitting, throughout the year, a sirloin of beef as a standing dish—not exiled to the side-table, but placed down before himself; and it was his pride and delight to help it, with all the heartiness and kindness of a true English merchant, whose whole object seemed to be, to make everybody under his roof welcome and happy.

Peregrine's *debut* at the dinner-table was

exceedingly successful ; he had quite sufficient *tact* to talk, when he could talk, well ; and upon subjects which he understood he made no inconsiderable figure. The moment the conversation turned upon anything which he did not happen in the slightest degree to comprehend, he became the most patient passive listener; his countenance expressing the strongest possible anxiety to obtain information ; but then, he sometimes went beyond that, and having fished out a point which he thought he could manage, he would try back upon it, and ask a question, most pertinent in its character, founded upon the information he had just picked up, and which, while it proved to the original holder-forth the attention which he had paid to what had passed, and the aptitude of his mind, impressed him with an idea that, in point of fact he knew a great deal more of the subject-matter under discussion, than he had at first admitted.

Peregrine, upon this occasion, did his best ; and as there was no stickling for precedence in

Nobbatop's house, he succeeded in getting himself placed between Mrs. Nobbatop and Maria,
and really made himself exceedingly agreeable.
If any fleeting recollections of Mrs. Mimminy,
Miss Lucetta, and Kitty Catheral, crossed his
mind for a moment, he drowned them in the
moussue champagne of his host, while he continued to keep the ladies "all alive," much to the
mystification of Mr. Nobbatop, who, though he
appeared to begin to recollect something about
him, and was quite sure that he deserved to be
where he was, because his wife and adopted
daughter told him so——determined that when
they retired to rest, he would make some further
inquiries of his lady into the history of his
acquaintance with him, and, if possible, as to
the place which he filled in society,——in fact,
to cut the matter short, to find out, as people
say, " *whom* he was, and *what* he was."

It has been the fashion for some years past,
for nobodies with fine houses, to get somebodies to invite anybodies and everybodies to

the nobodies' parties ; and even in the regular
routine of society, without such extraordinary
efforts to do something, there does not happen
a ball in London, during the season, at which
the master of the house is just as little acquainted with a dozen or two, or the dancing
men of the evening, as Nobbatop was with
Peregrine Bunce. Peregrine, however, was
located—his bed was ready—his dressing-room-
fire was lighted—his toilet spread—his clothes
were laid out—his servant was in waiting, and
he was in fact domiciled ; so that the inquiry,
unless in the hurry of business his host happened
to forget all about it, was not very important.

Mr. Nobbatop did not, however, forget ; and
when in the sanctified seclusion of the marital
chamber he and his lady talked over the events
of the day past, and of the proposed arrangements of the day to come, Nobbatop received so
favourable and satisfactory an account of our
hero, and of his agreeable manners, various
accomplishments, and rich uncle, that the

worthy merchant, whose happiness, as we have already said, consisted in making those happy who were round him, suggested to his better half an extension of the invitation to their new guest, and the expression to *him* of a hope that he would stay the week with them.

Mr. Nobbatop was off for the city long before his family or visitors made their appearance at the breakfast-table ; but certainly never were more honied words distilled into the ears of Mr. Peregrine Bunce, than those which, from the ruby lips of Maria Grayson, announced that her aunt was going to beg him to favour them with his company for a few days. Mrs. Nobbatop had imparted the fact to her niece, and the reader is left to decide upon the nature of Maria's feelings towards Peregrine, after being told that she was too much pleased, to deprive her aunt of the opportunity of imparting the invitation to their guest, and to be the bearer of it herself.

There is in this world no happiness without

alloy ; and although Peregrine found himself all at once received, invited, *fêted* and encouraged, not only by the heads of the house, but by the object of his ambition, his else unqualified delight was moderated down into something like regret, that he had not known the real state of the family circumstances, as regarded the supposed engagement between her and her cousin, when he was there before. Then, all the provoking intercourse with the Mintons would have been avoided—then, all the exposure with the widow Mimminy would never have taken place ; nor, calculating as he did, that in the supposed case of his success with Maria Grayson, some months before, would Miss Katherine Catheral have been in England to bring herself and her calamities to his notice, until at all events it would have been too late to prevent the marriage.

To persons not in public life, and unaccustomed (as *they* are) to the constant exhibition of their names, as a matter of course, in every day's newspaper, the appearance in the columns of what are genteelly called the daily and weekly journals, of the patronymic of an ordinary steady-going individual, is something startling ; and however anxious a young author, or a young anything, is to see himself in print, all the world ——save and except the care-burdened classes, who are used to it——feel a nervousness and a sort of strange sensation at seeing themselves published by name in the columns of the Times, Post, Herald, or Chronicle, as the case may be——and this nervousness is observable even in the people who have themselves, by their own confidential servants, paid their seven shillings for the express purpose of being be-paragraphed and be-puffed.

When such is the case, the patient invariably reads the one paragraph about himself over and over again fifty times : the name Hobkírk, or Puddephat, or whatever it is, in which he rejoices, looks larger than any other word in the column before his eyes ; and he sits and gazes on it with a mingled delight and apprehension——

delight at finding it there—qualified by a false punctuation, wrong spelling, or a mistaken distinction—and the apprehension, that he may be laughed at for his self-exaltation.

Different is it, when, without the previous soothing process, some editorial remark brings the " private individual" before the public gaze —the restlessness—the anxiety of the unfortunate victim, who believes that everybody has read *that* which perhaps nobody has even seen; and that the eyes of a whole party are consequently turned upon him, while most probably he is personally unknown to the whole collection of lookers-on.

But far different were Peregrine Bunce's apprehensions—To be noticed in the " Chit-chat," or the " Fashionable intelligence," would not in the slightest degree have displeased *him ;* and an announcement, that he had left the Ship Hotel at Brighton, for London, would probably have been thrice read and once pointed out to Miss Grayson, whose possible innocence of the fact, that all such reports must originate either with the fashionable removers themselves, their servants, or the waiters at the hotels where they put up, might have measured Peregrine's importance by the notice taken of him in public papers.

None of this, however, was acting upon Peregrine—his dread was, not of seeing himself so announced; but of seeing himself, as Kitty Catheral had threatened, advertised—with a " Whereas Mr. Peregrine Bunce," at the head of the advertisement, setting forth in its body the cruel desertion of the said Catherine by the said Peregrine. Suppose such a thing to occur just at the moment when the bright sun shone, and the path was strewed with flowers. And then he began to consider, and ask himself, whether he had adopted a wise course in setting this unfortunate but now infuriated girl at defiance; and it would be very difficult indeed adequately to represent or describe the state of his feelings, as the two or three daily papers, which made their appearance regularly on the

breakfast-table, (when no very particular accident interfered,) per railroad, every morning.

Maria Grayson has been in some sort described to the reader—but not quite clearly
enough; she was very quick, and clever—without
the slightest pretension to a pedestal; but sharp
in conversation, quite good enough in music
not to be a bore, either as to the badness of her
performance, or its excellence, she played and
sang if she were asked, and sang nicely too—
never attempting things unattainable by her
powers. She drew, and well enough for all she
wanted;—if her houses *were* a little out of the
perpendicular, her clouds a little like apple-dump-
lings, and her trees a little like Bishops' wigs of
the olden time, elevated upon pitch-forks, she
drew from nature. She knew nothing of geology,
nor of any other ology, nor did she write
billets-doux, in Greek; but she was quite fit
to fill her station in a drawing-room, and to
take her part in conversation—ready to oblige—
willing to dance with a little boy, if it were for

the benefit of society, or to play the quadrilles in which her associates were to show off. In fact, for Peregrine, Maria was just the wife; and happy was it for him that she seemed to think that *he* was just the husband for *her*.

She was very handsome; and, as we have already said, had been much run after. She thought, however, that she knew more of the world than she really did know; and having chilled the aspiring dandies of the army because she looked upon them as fortune-hunters, turned towards Peregrine, not only because she preferred him personally, but because she was quite sure he was *not* mercenary—thus reminding one of the mouse in the fable, that fled in terror from the cock, which it saw strutting and crowing about the farm-yard, to place its confidence in the sleek tabby Tom, by whose plain coat and apparently gentle manners the poor little innocent had been completely beguiled.

To get at as much of Peregrine's feelings as he chose to communicate, and at all events to

appreciate his own view of his position, perhaps
we may as well conclude this chapter with a
letter, which he wrote on the Tuesday evening,
in his first week's sojourn at Mr. Nobbatop's, to
his uncle :—

> " *Stambury Park,*
> " ——, *Nov.* ——, 18——.

" MY DEAR UNCLE,

   " When I left you and London, I was so
very uncertain as to my next *pied à terre,* that
I did not attempt to give you the power of
writing to *me,* from my own ignorance as to the
place to which you could address me.

   " I am, as you will see by the date of this,
most comfortably housed, for a week clear, in a
very delightful family, who are kind and obliging
beyond measure. I am sure you have heard me
speak of them last year, as exceedingly agreeable people ; but it is only when one actually
lives domesticated with friends, that a man can
perfectly understand or duly appreciate them.

   " My host is the head of the famous house of

Nobbatop, Snaggs, and Widdlebury, and is one of the most amiable and at the same time sound-headed men I ever met with——indefatigable in business, of which he seems a complete master ; he leaves home by eight o'clock in the morning at the latest, and does not return till just dinner-time——his knowledge of mercantile matters is quite surprising ; and all I should fear would be, except that he allows himself relaxation on Sundays, that he would overwork his mind, and, as I should say, break down.

" His wife is everything that a merchant's wife of the highest *grade* should be——perfectly unaffected, and friendly, almost amounting to what one might call motherly as to her domestic arrangements ; she receives all her neighbours, who are too glad to be attentive to her, with an equality of civility and kindness, which might serve as a lesson for those who are, as regards society, much her superiors.

" Her son, who is at present absent, and about

to be married, I remember liking exceedingly, but I always imagined him engaged to the divinity of this shrine — Miss Grayson, one of the most engaging girls I ever met with ; lively and playful, yet full of simplicity and diffidence, the best-natured creature that ever lived ; exceedingly handsome, with bright black eyes, and forty or fifty thousand pounds. She is the niece and adopted daughter of mine host, who has invited me to stay here throughout the week.

" The place is charming for a modern villa ; it might perhaps pretend to more—it has a portico, through which you enter a handsome hall, surrounded by a gallery leading to various bed-rooms — a saloon of some forty feet by thirty faces you—on one side of the hall is an admirable dinner-room, and on the other a small drawing-room and library—beyond the dining-room is the billiard-room, communicating with what I call the saloon, but which, in fact, is the general living room—the whole thing is done in the best possible style.   His stables are good—his cellar perfect; and I do think, considering all things, I have been most fortunate in coming hither.

' When goes he hence ?'

says Lady Macbeth, speaking of Duncan—talking of myself, I could as easily answer the question as Duncan's murderer. It strikes me that mine will prove an elastic invitation indeed, and that, as the marriage of young Nobbatop is so soon to take place, I *may* be retained here, even till the celebration of that ceremony.

" If ever there were a girl calculated to make a man perfectly happy, I do think, from all I have seen of her during our very short association, I should say it was Maria Grayson. You cannot imagine anything more delightful than her manner—such frankness and good humour, such appreciation of anything said to her. I declare, my dear Uncle, that the forty or fifty thousand pounds, which they say she has, has no more effect upon my feelings towards her, than so many grains of sand.

" Suffice it to say, that here I should be perfectly happy, if I were certain as to the measures
proposed to be taken by that vixen Kitty Catheral.
At present I am greatly obliged to her for having
broken off a match between me and a driveller,
which, in point of fact, the widow was—with all
her absurdities about rams, turkeys, and pug-
dogs; and as for the daughter, I defy any man,
father-in-law or whatever he might be, to keep
her out of the way of mischief; she was born to
it, and, mark my word, will, (if she have not
already done so,) fulfil her destiny.

" I should like very much to hear from you,
whether you are aware of any further proceedings of Miss Catheral; but I scarcely know
how to desire you to write to me here, because, if any accident or delay in the post, or
your absence from town, should postpone your
answer, so that it should arrive here after I
was gone, it might give the Nobbatops an idea
that I had proposed myself as a fixture. Therefore, my dear Uncle, if you have anything to

say, and will be kind enough to say it, direct to me, ' Post Office, Thames Ditton—to be left till called for.' Any information will, I assure you, be thankfully received.

" If I can but get clear, even for a few weeks, of the Catheral affair, I am safe ; for here, my dearest Uncle, all seems plain sailing, and no doubts or difficulties.—This may sound vain, but in this case I think, as the London raffs say, ' There is *no* mistake.'

" Believe me, my dear Uncle,

" Your affectionate Nephew,

" PEREGRINE BUNCE."

CHAPTER XIV.

IT may readily be supposed, that Uncle Noll was
highly gratified with Peregrine's representation
of his then present position, and congratulated
himself upon the vast improvement in his prospects, and the rapidity with which they had
opened to his view.   Like his nephew, he certainly did feel a little apprehensive that more
would be heard of the irate and ungentle Kitty;
and with all his anxiety to prevent any unpleasant exposure, he did not clearly see how he
could manage to do so.   If he called at the
lodgings which Peregrine had abdicated, to
make any inquiries whether such a person had
herself, or by proxy, applied there, since his

departure, it might rather whet the appetite of
the landlord's curiosity——or that of his wife——
and moreover might, if the visit were repeated,
induce the dissatisfied damsel to consider herself of more importance than she really was; and
still further, as the said landlord was aware of
Uncle Noll's place of residence in London, it
might induce her to visit the Tavistock Hotel,
accompanied by her attorney and his asso- .
ciates.

Peregrine himself was, as we know, exceedingly cunning and cautious, and, as he believed,
had cut the connexion with his lodgings so
dexterously, that not a thread remained which
could, by any possibility, serve as a clue to his
present retreat ; but Peregrine had forgotten,
that however anxious for secrecy and seclusion
he himself might be, and however important
they were to him while shirking his duty towards an unfortunate young woman, his servant
Tim was not placed in a similar predicament ;
on the contrary, having engaged the affections of

the daughter of the ostler *en-chef* at the livery
stables, where his master's horses stood, he had
resolved, whenever the proper time arrived,
to marry the said daughter ; so that hereafter
when the head ostler should have succeeded to
the then master, *he* might become head ostler,
and when the master, being then his father-in-
law, should " shuffle off this mortal coil," he
should eventually succeed to the mastership.

And all this course was running smoothly. It
was with the ostler's consent the courtship had
been going on, and it was understood in the
family, that whenever Tim should have cheated
his master out of as much as his respectable
future father-in-law thought sufficient for a start
in life, he should marry the girl ; the marriage
being also dependent upon another contingency ;
that is to say, the succession of her father to
the occupancy of the stables on his own account, which would, in a similar way, with the
previously described arrangement depend upon
his success in cheating *his* master to an extent

sufficient to enable him to pay for his lease and good-will.

Under this honourable and satisfactory understanding between the parties, it was merely natural that Mr. Peregrine Bunce's servant Tim and his sweetheart should keep up a proper and constant correspondence. Peregrine never took the precaution of warning Tim not to say whither they were gone, for two reasons ; first, because he did not, in his slyness, think it prudent to make a confidant of his servant; and, secondly, because he had no idea that he was likely to enter into a correspondence with any friend in London.

Unfortunately, however, for Peregrine, there *was* this correspondence progressing, as the Americans say, between the ostler's daughter and Tim, who, thanks to the march of intellect ! which elevates the mind, and exalts the human character, was in the daily, or, as he would perhaps have called it, the " every-other-daily," habit of writing to his Dulcinea.

It so happened, that one of the most active inquirers after Peregrine, at his late lodgings, Mr. Hobsnob, Kitty Catheral's attorney, took it into his head to inquire of the landlord where Mr. Bunce kept his horses, when he was in London.   The landlord of the house told him as a matter of course.   Hobsnob lost no time in ferreting out the fact ; and seeing the dear Eloisa Jane Scruff, the betrothed of Tim, in the balcony of the stable-yard, enticed her down by saying that he had something of the greatest importance to Mr. Peregrine Bunce's interest to mention, but did not know where to find him.

The plump and jolly Eloisa Jane was caught in the snare.   Unconscious would she have been under any circumstances, then, of the mischief which her communicativeness might cause ; and down she came, and gave Hobsnob the direction to the present residence of Peregrine, copied from Tim's last letter.

The little boy at the oilman's, who was sent

down into the cellar to draw some beer, and stuck his candle into an open barrel of gunpowder, which he fancied rape-seed, while he performed the operation, was not more unconscious of the probable consequences of his proceeding, than was the unsuspicious girl at the livery stables of her's. And here it may not be out of place to record the presence of mind of that said oilman under the circumstances—the boy came up with the beer, having left the candle below—

" Where is the candle?" said the master.

" Dear me," said the boy, " I forgot the candle—I've left it sticking in the open barrel of rape-seed in the cellar."

The oilman knew what the barrel really contained;——he, his wife, and children, were seated at supper in a parlour immediately over the cellar—death and destruction to all of them must follow if the slightest doubt or shaking of a hand in removing the candle caused a single spark to fall; conscious of his own incapacity to

take it from its place without tremor—assured
that one word of communication on the subject
would scatter the family and endanger the
existence of them all, he, with a power of mind
calculated assuredly for greater things, said to
the boy—" Well, then, go and fetch it up."

The boy, wholly inapprehensive of consequences, did as he was bid, went down and took
out the candle as steadily as he had put it into
the barrel, and sure enough, as they say, *did*
bring it up. Just consider the feelings of the
father of that family during the minute or so
which was consumed in the boy's return to the
cellar—think what he must have endured, as he
heard him trudge down the stairs, " whistling as
he went for want of thought,"—he sat, as it
were, paralysed — he listened — he heard him
coming up again—he saw him with the light in
his hand safe before him. Then it was that he
burst into a flood of tears, fell on his knees, and
thanked Heaven for the deliverance of himself
and family.

This anecdote, which is truth, may be liable
to critical remark ; and the historian may be
sneered at, as the panegyrist of a sentimental
pickle-man ; but knowing the circumstances,
and duly appreciating the instant resolution of
the hero, he risks the chance of ridicule, to do
justice to wisdom and fortitude, where justice
is due.

Miss Eloisa Jane's performance, however,
turned out unfortunately in a very different manner. The candle which she had unconsciously
stuck——not exactly into a barrel of rape-seed——
but the light which she had most unfortunately
thrown upon Peregrine's retreat, produced, as
the reader may already anticipate, a *blow-up*,
which, if not so fatal in the way of life and
limb as that which was threatened at the oil-
shop, was fraught with results the least possibly
pleasant to our worthy friend Mr. Peregrine
Bunce.

It was about four days after Mr. Hobsnob
had received the desired information, and about

the fourth day of Peregrine's domestication at Slambury—so was the domicile of Mr. Nobbatop named—that as Peregrine, just waiting for luncheon, was sitting *vis-à-vis* to Miss Maria Grayson, with his hands extended, so that she might, in the most convenient and agreeable manner to herself, wind off from his fingers on to a sort of reel, a skein of deep-green silk, intended, as she told him, " if he behaved well," to form part of a purse which she graciously designed to make him, a servant came into the room, and hinted, in a gentle whisper, that a gentleman wished to speak to him, and that he—the servant—had shown the gentleman into the library.

" Me !" said Peregrine—somewhat agitated, and feeling himself get pale all at once—" *Me !* —are you sure ?—it is'nt my uncle—I expect nobody else—just say that I am engaged at the moment—and ask the gentleman to send in his name."

The servant of course did as he was ordered,

and Peregrine went on being wound from, but his hand was by no means steadied by the announcement, although, in all his surmises and calculations, it so happened that he did not hit upon the right subject of annoyance.

The man returned just as the reeling and winding were concluded, and told Peregrine that the gentleman said Mr. Bunce did not know him by name, but that he would not detain him ten minutes.

" Will you forgive me?" said Peregrine, gallantly, to Maria Grayson ; " the worst of being much in society is, that a man can go nowhere without being hunted."

" That," said Maria, graciously, " is the inevitable result of popularity."

To describe the feelings which operated upon our friend Peregrine during his passage to the library would indeed be exceedingly difficult. His thoughts flew about with a perilous quickness, and had not settled to any definite point, when, opening the door of the room, he saw,

walking up and down with a measured step, a
sort of shabby-genteel, sickly-looking, smooth-
faced, well-shorn person, unknown to him by
sight, wearing a black coat and waistcoat, and
sorrel-coloured shorts, with gaiters to match.
His salutation of Peregrine was not at all calculated to induce him to believe that he felt any
particular respect for him ; but as the visitor's
hair grew lengthily behind, and hung over a very
greasy collar, Peregrine hoped at the first blush,
that he was a roving missionary, or perhaps a
collector for some mistaken set of people, who
club their money to do more mischief in their
own time, than all the energies of their progeny
will ever be able to repair.

However, Peregrine bowed very civilly —
meaning by his manner to say, " What do you
happen to want ?"

" You, Sir," said the stranger, " are Mr.
Bunce, I presume?"

" Exactly so," said Peregrine.

" My business, Sir," said the stranger, " is

not altogether agreeable ; but I have no doubt we shall very shortly come to an understanding."

" May I ask your name, Sir ?" said Peregrine.

" My name, Sir, is Hobsnob," answered the stranger.

" And the business ?"

" Why, Sir," said Hobsnob—for Hobsnob it was—" is merely to ask your intentions with regard to the payment of certain bills for which a client of mine, Miss Katherine Catheral, remains up to this moment liable, but which, upon what is called an honourable understanding between you, you have agreed to pay."

" Oh !" said Peregrine, drawing himself up, and feeling, on the first impulse of the moment, the organ of kickitaveness very much excited ; —" if *that* is your business Sir, you may go— my mind is made up."

" Well, Sir," said Hobsnob—who moved no muscle of his cadaverous face, and who talked

exactly as a methodist preacher, with what the
children call the mulligrubs, would have doled
out his words,—" other persons have made up
their minds too.   Miss Catheral is acting upon
my advice, and, in fact, the business I have
with you here, is to serve you personally—for
she did not wish you to be annoyed—with a
writ—a copy of which I have in my breeches
pocket."

" A writ ! Sir," said Peregrine, still doing
brave ;—" a writ for what, Sir ?—what am I to
do with a writ, Sir ?"

" Anything you please, Sir," said Hobsnob ;
" I would much rather, for your sake, the
matter should be compromised, although, I dare
say I need not tell you, it will be more to my
advantage that it should go to trial."

" Trial, Sir!" said Peregrine ; " what do you
mean by talking to me of trial ?—you know that
I am not legally responsible—that I cannot be
sued for these bills, and even if I could, and
it comes to *that*, Sir, I would go upon the im-

morality of the connexion, and so drive you out
of court—as it is, you hav'n't a leg to stand
upon."

" You seem to know something of the law,
Sir," said the small attorney, " and probably
you may be right—but we *will* try it ; although,
I assure you, my personal visit here has been
occasioned, as I have told you before, by a desire
to prevent exposure."

" Exposure !" said Peregrine, standing with
his back to the chimney-piece ; " who cares for
exposure, Sir ?—don't imagine that anything
like a threat will affect *me*—I think the application extremely improper, and your inter-
ference wholly uncalled for, and all I can say
is ——" (and here Peregrine stuck the poker
into the fire)—" that I am not the man to be
bullied or imposed upon."

" I did not come here," said the immoveable,
plausible pettifogger, " to bully or impose upon
you. I came to appeal to you, and to put it

to you, whether it would not be better to stay proceedings, than have this affair reported in all the newspapers?"

Now Peregrine undoubtedly thought, as the attorney professed to think; but he thought also, that, by showing a bold front to the enemy, he might succeed in putting the affair at rest at once. The idea of the general publication of the case, well put in by the paltry practitioner, nevertheless had its effect.

"Well," said Peregrine, "supposing I *were* fool enough to listen to terms, what would be the amount?"

"I should say," answered Hobsnob, contracting his brows, compressing his lips, and casting his eyes upwards, as if such a fellow either expected to get anything from heaven, or go thither himself,——"I should say somewhere about four hundred pounds would cover all."

"Four hundred what?" said Peregrine, giving

the poker, just then rapidly reaching a red heat, another turn,—" why, I would see you and the ———"

" Don't put yourself in a passion, Sir," said the attorney; " I am only acting for another person, and I must conscientiously do my duty ———."

" Conscientiously!" said Peregrine.

" And," continued the lawyer, " my hope was, that I might have been prevented the necessity of executing this service."

" Service, Sir," said Peregrine ; " why, I will defend the case, or rather the no case, to the last extremity, as I have told you ; you have admitted that I know the law, and, moreover, I defy you, or any of your myrmidons, to produce one scrap of paper upon which I ever rendered myself liable for the unfortunate person by whom you are employed."

" I see, Sir," said Hobsnob, " you are irritated ; and I think with you, perhaps, that it may be as well for me to abstain from taking the step which I at first intended. It is quite clear, that with some minds, persuasion, and a mild and moderate appeal, have a more powerful effect than coercion. My client, Miss Katherine Catheral, is now at the Swan at Ditton, to which inn she accompanied me, and I think—as she tells me she *has* frequently seen the worthy lady of this house, when she was engaged as governess in a family near Guildford, it *is* possible that a personal appeal to your better feelings, aided by the countenance of the excellent Mrs. Nobbatop, may effect that object, which, with a generally existing prejudice against legal proceedings, you at present utterly repel. As that is the case, Sir, I will, upon my own responsibility, withhold the service, and Miss Catheral and myself will be here between eleven and twelve to-morrow."

A thunderbolt hurled by the hand of Jove himself could not have more effectually demolished Mr. Peregrine Bunce: pulling the poker out of the fire, he requested—for the first time —Mr. Hobsnob to sit down.

" Will you take any refreshment?" said Peregrine.

" No, Sir, thank you," replied the attenuated attorney.

" It would be a pity," said Peregrine, " to bring you over here again to-morrow."

" Not the least trouble," said Hobsnob; " visits of business always go into the bill of costs.—It seems to be very fine air here. I don't care how often I attend you."

" But I do," thought Peregrine.

" And so," said he, " Miss Catheral is at Ditton. How did she know that I had been at Ditton?"

" I hav'n't the slightest idea, Sir," said Hobsnob.

" It is very strange," said Peregrine.

" Very, Sir," said Hobsnob,—" but with regard to business, what am I to say to my client?

—will one o'clock to-morrow suit you better than twelve ?"

" Why," said Peregrine, " I was thinking it would be best to save all that unnecessary trouble—you must know, Mr. Snob —— "

" Hobsnob," said the mummy, bowing his head, and attempting a smile.

" —— Mr. Hobsnob— I beg pardon—you must know that in matters of this sort everything ought to be left to feeling. Heaven knows that I entertain but one sentiment towards poor dear Kitty—and the last thing I could endure upon earth would be to hear of her being worried or inconvenienced in her circumstances ; but established as she is —— "

" Pardon me, Sir," said Hobsnob ; " that is a point to which I have not *yet* come;—ruined as she is by her last exposure at Brighton, the chances are, that she never can regain her footing — certainly not amongst the class of persons with whom she has been hitherto engaged."

" Well, well," said Peregrine, who was exceedingly alarmed lest his companion should talk loud, or that the ladies might linger in the hall, into which one of the doors of the library opened,—" Well, well, we won't discuss *that*— all I can say is, that with *me* law is needless ; the dictates of my own heart and feelings are what I invariably act upon ; and I assure you, my dear Sir,—and so I call you, perhaps, too familiarly, because you take an interest in Kitty, —that it was simply the idea, that she had recourse to legal means to force me into doing what it was always my inclination and intention to do, that drove me to set up a defence, which, with your gentlemanly principles, you must be certain I never could have intended seriously to maintain."

" I assure you, Sir," said Hobsnob, " I am exceedingly glad to hear this explanation ; and I think our business may be brought into a nut-shell."

" What !" said Peregrine, boiling with rage,

indignation, and every other base passion that could agitate a cold, selfish heart,—" What *is* really the sum which will make the poor dear girl comfortable, and put her entirely at her ease ?"

" Why," said the attorney, who saw how completely he had hooked his fish,—" I stated just now, what I thought would be the probable expenses if the case went to trial, but then I spoke professionally ; you have most generously abandoned that style of conversation, and I put it to your liberality—Give me a cheque on her account for four hundred pounds, and I will pledge myself that you never will be troubled more on her account."

" If I would," said Peregrine, " I could not at this moment ; but if you will trust me so far, I have no objection this instant to give you an I O U for the amount, which, the very day after I return to town, I will take up."

" That, Sir," said Hobsnob, " is perfectly satisfactory ; and, to show you how disinterest-

edly anxious I am in this affair, direct the
I O U to Miss Catheral—I mean, say at foot
of it,—' To Miss Katherine Catheral;' for, as
you know little of *me*, without that caution, I
might—not that I say I should—appropriate it
to my own use—or it might be lost—or a thousand things might occur." Hobsnob, of course,
never meant that Kitty should see the " docu-
ment," for her doing which, as he represented *her*,
and would shortly re-present the paper to Peregrine, there could not be the slightest necessity.
The proposition, however, involved a show of
integrity, which, as it cost him nothing, the
worthy " gent." thought it wise to make.

Never were three letters penned by man more
painfully, than the ominous vowels which pre-
ceded the numeral four hundred : however, it
was done, and Mr. Hobsnob was bowed out;
took his departure never, as Peregrine hoped,
to return, and proceeded to Ditton, to inform
Miss Catheral, (that is to say, if she really were
there,) of the success of his mission.

G 2

Peregrine, enraptured at having got rid of him upon any terms, returned to the ladies, muttering to himself, with Macbeth——

" So, being gone, I am a man again ! "

" Well, Mr. Bunce," said Maria, as Peregrine re-entered the morning room, " your friend kept you an amazingly long time ; and Mama and I think we ought to make all sorts of apologies for not sending to you, to beg him to stay and have some luncheon."

" Oh, dear, no ! " said Peregrine ; " it was one of my tradesmen, who was anxious to take my orders about something he has to do for me."

" What ! " said Mrs. Nobbatop, looking up from her work ; " are you going, as they say, to change your condition ? "

" I wish I were," said Peregrine ; " but I am one of the universally rejected of young ladies."

" Fishing for compliments, Mr. Bunce," said

Maria, looking just as he must have wished her to look.

"Not I," said Bunce. "If I went after such sport, I fancy my success wouldn't be much better than with the barbel at Ditton."

"I don't mind your bad sport there," said Maria; "for, perhaps, if you had been exceedingly fortunate with the barbel, we might not have been lucky enough to keep you here so long."

Oh! if anybody capable of appreciating Peregrine's feelings, which we hope few people are, how readily will they understand the joy, the rapture, the almost shuddering delight, with which he heard these words. To hear a young and handsome creature, placed, as *she* was, in the midst of wealth and luxury, express her joy at his being associated with her; it was something even beyond his highest hopes—or, as the cockneys would write it, "aspirations;"—he bowed his head—looked his uttermost—and said—

G 3

" Miss Grayson, you will make me too vain."

" No," said Maria, " I want to make nobody vain. I have been brought up in the school of truth, and have no disguises : my aunt here knows my opinion of you, for I conceal nothing from her, and *she* knows that I like your society; and that being the case, I really do not see why I should affect not to like it ; so then, liking it, is it but natural that we——for my aunt and I are perfectly *d'accord* upon this point—should be extremely glad to have you amongst us in our quiet family-party?"

" You see, Mr. Bunce," said Mrs. Nobba-top, " my dear child, as I call and consider her, speaks plainly : it is the custom of our house—we affect nothing—we are content with the truth ; and if my dear husband could but manage to divert his mind and attention a little more than he does from his numerous avoca-tions in the city, I know you would like him better than you do, and it would be much better for himself."

" Indeed," said Peregrine, "however much I may agree with you, as to the necessity of his relaxation from such intense business, no such process is necessary to increase the esteem, and, I might almost say, affection, which I at present feel for him."

" You were born to be a courtier, Mr. Bunce," said Maria ; " you are the best ' complimenter,' if there be such a word in the dictionary, I ever met with. Your civil things are said so *apropos*, and come in so naturally, that one is almost inclined to fancy you sincere."

" I hope, Miss Grayson," said Peregrine, looking as if he were acting Joseph Surface in the School for Scandal, " that I am never *in*-sincere ;—why should I be ?—in this house it would be impossible, for I have every ——"

" There, there," interrupted Mrs. Nobbatop; " don't take the trouble to answer Maria's pertnesses ; if I ever *did* tell secrets, I could let you know ——"

" Aunt," almost screamed Maria, " what *are* you going to say ?"

" Something," said Mrs. Nobbatop, " which you would not at all mind Mr. Bunce's hearing."

" What that is, I don't know," said Maria; " but—but—suppose we go to luncheon——we have been only waiting for *you*."

Bunce looked at Maria, saw her confusion and even blushes, and heard the tremulousness of her voice, when she proposed the adjournment. — He was satisfied—' *Veni, vidi, vici,*'—the affair was settled. Short as had been his domestication at the hall, or house, or park, or whatever it was called, he had unquestionably carried his point, and *that* too with the evident sanction and approbation of the amiable Mrs. Nobbatop herself.

CHAPTER XV.

THERE is certainly nothing in the world so unequivocally delightful, as the self-satisfied feeling which a gentleman, " on promotion," enjoys when he becomes conscious that he has made his hit; and Peregrine was not flattering himself too much when he enjoyed this most agreeable conviction—he *had* made his hit. Maria Grayson was certainly one of the most unaffected girls that ever lived; with eloquent eyes, and a power of attractiveness which a man could no more describe than resist, but which, perhaps, anybody who has seen a half-languishing, half-laughing brunette, in whose countenance so much more was expressed than words, however ably written, could convey, may understand. The arched brow — the playful mouth—the one pet mole on the cheek—and the dimple which grew there, as if by magic, when she smiled—the affected frown, when she thought it right to repress the liveliness of her companion, and the assumed gravity if Mama caught something in the way of playfulness, which she thought a little *too* playful, were all charming in their way. In his case, to speak truth, Peregrine *had* made his lodgement in the lady's heart.

In the days of Richardson, it became essential to such a reciprocity, that the heart should not only be touched, but captured. In these our more modern times, when sentiment is as entirely excluded from ordinary society, as hoops and swords, (and, *par parenthèse*, sentimentality so decked out seems droll,) it does not appear at all necessary that anything like desperation or desolation should follow as the natural consequences of a rejected suit, although it certainly does follow, that a pining miss, or a desponding beau, would, in these days, be two objects of immeasurable ridicule in all the salons of the season, the thresholds of which, neither sympathy nor sensibility, ever presumes to cross.

N'importe—here we have *our* two—our pair —Peregrine devoted, and Maria doomed; and no state of things could be more comfortable for both of them—for, as it seemed, they liked each other extremely, and those who happened to drop in during the week, would, and probably might, have justly said, they loved.

O Uncle Noll, Uncle Noll—here *was* a consummation by you so devoutly wished!—here were beauty, talent, fortune, accomplishments, all concentred, gained, captivated, and captured, in less than a fortnight after the most signal defeat that a Lothario ever encountered. Here was no show of tender affection—no word of passion—it seemed as if by a mutual understanding, Peregrine and the girl had got over all the cold and doubtful preliminaries, and that without one syllable having been spoken, they understood each other, and that the affair had been settled after what the sweet poet calls—

" The full-grown Adam"

Fashion.—But that is the way in which nine marriages out of ten are brought about : it is the liking produced by social intercourse—or what I have elsewhere quoted from Miss Edgeworth, " juxta-position,"—it is the habit. Peregrine could make himself extremely agreeable ; but it should be observed, (as it has been often observed, how lucky it is that everybody does not admire the same object) that what is extremely agreeable to one person or one set of people, is excessively disagreeable, and even disgusting, to another.

In one circle you will find a forward pretender to all things, howling out songs, serious and comic ;—dancing, and talking (with an affectation of ridiculing it) slang and vulgarity ; considered the most charming and entertaining

creature in all the world. Take him next door
to the house in which he is so prized, and the
chances are, the groom of the chambers will
be ordered to show him the door in ten
minutes. Go to another place, and there you
will see a proser of the dullest order drawling
out poetry, or talking fine—which, by the way, is
the lowest of all vulgarities—who is gazed upon
by the coterie as something exceedingly charming, who would not get admission into the hall
of the house, in which the vivacious bore, just
alluded to, is a leader.——This is fortunate.

> " These things are matters of opinion ;
> Some *loves* an apple—some an *inion*."

And if it were *not* so, society would be " confusion worse confounded :" all the world would
be running after one object——everybody would
be ravenous for one dish ; and some one wine
would be so universally drunk, that there would
be a great and affecting drought upon the face
of the earth.

Peregrine was never slow at availing himself of circumstances and contingencies likely to be available in his pursuits ; and he calculated with no slight degree of judgment and discrimination, that the now rapidly approaching marriage of Mr. George Nobbatop with Miss Screecher, of Caddington, would not only justify sundry apposite allusions to the happiness of the married state, but even, if he could get the business sufficiently forward, give a sort of opening for a suggestion, that if Maria Grayson really *did* feel, as he was confident she did, an affection for him ; there might be that which in some families is considered an agreeable thing — a double marriage ; so that on the same day upon which Miss Screecher became Mrs. Nobbatop, Miss Grayson might become Mrs. Bunce.

This thought having entered and taken possession of his mind, Peregrine resolved to follow up the suggestion ; and although the season of the year was avowedly unfavourable to the evening walks and moon-light strolls, during which amatory proceedings are best carried on; where, when words are wanting, and twilight hides the blushes of the consenting girl, the genuine feeling of the heart is practically confessed; still he thought, if he could contrive to catch her alone, and attract her thoughts to the point of her cousin's marriage, that would be the moment to " pop," as Uncle Noll had it. Else the playfulness and naturalness (as the cockneys say) of Maria Grayson's manner were such that he utterly despaired of making her think him serious and in earnest. Besides, the period of their acquaintance had been so short.

Well! but then she was so ingenuous, so lively, so gay, so tender, so affectionate.——If any thing occurred in conversation which brought him or his pursuits, or his prospects, forward——what could he do?——make a dash at once——stand not upon the order of popping, but pop, justify some sudden act of devotion by the force of his passion, and the rapture of delight with which

he was inflamed. No—it was too soon for
that—and yet there was a Captain of Lancers
who went a good way a-head of him in his
attentions during the morning, now and then ;
but *he* was never asked to dinner ; and so poor
Peregrine doubted—should he, or should he not
do something decisive and deciding ?—No, he
resolved to bide his time—remain another week
if he were invited, ingratiate himself still more
as a friend, and then suddenly throw off his dis-
guise like Sheridan's beef-eater, and all at once
proclaim himself the lover.

Peregrine became under the sheltering roof
of Mr. Nobbatop, not only a special pet with
the ladies of the house, but succeeded in giving
several of the visitors, who partook of the daily
dinners which graced his hospitable board, an
exceedingly favourable opinion of his qualities.
Wholly abstracted, as we have before said, in
his mercantile pursuits, all that Nobbatop
sought or required was, that his family should
be happy, and that when he returned from the

fatigues of business he should find an agreeable, but small——else would it not have been
agreeable——party, assembled to partake of his
excellent fare.

Amongst others of the occasional visitors at
Slambury was a Mr. Towsey, to whom Peregrine
particularly " cottoned." He was a little man
——youngish, but shaped rather like an oil-jar——
with a round white face,——having, moreover, a
sort of Grimaldi tuft of reddish sandy hair on
the top of his head, and a feeble attempt at
whiskers under a pair of very large ears. He
was incalculably good-tempered, and by no
means without ability,——and, moreover, an out-
and-out sportsman,——came frequently to luncheon, fully equipped for what the French call
La Chasse, and was mightily affected towards
Maria Grayson.

This it was that so much interested Peregrine——this was why he cultivated his acquaintance. He felt sure that he had nothing to fear
from *him ;* and knew, moreover, that Maria's

whole object in paying him certain little attentions when he was present, was to convert his credulous reception of her well-feigned civilities into ridicule as soon as he was gone, illustrated and finished up by an imitation of his mental and personal attractions, with which the said Miss Maria Grayson would oceasionally favour the little family-circle when he had taken his departure.

During the period of Peregrine's probation, nobody can question the nervousness by which he must have been regularly affected touching the very uncertain means he had taken to soothe Kitty Catheral and-her friend. A woman angry, and naturally angry, at the sneaking desertion of her betrayer, is not a being easily to be subdued ; but when she confides her wrongs and demands of right to a dirty attorney, the case becomes perilous. For three shillings and four-pence the needy vampyre wou'd sacrifice his dearest friend—and for six-and-eightpence, sell his own soul. Such a creature was this Hobsnob—an animal, who, having persuaded the misguided girl to trust to *him*, had resolved, if he could threaten, bully, or alarm Peregrine into giving the I O U for four hundred pounds, to compromise with all the creditors with one hundred, give poor Kitty somewhere about twenty pounds for herself, pocket the rest, and perhaps affect genteel with his miserable family, and give a dance by way of a showing off of his great prosperity in his profession.

Peregrine certainly felt that he was displaying himself on the tight rope, so long as Hobsnob had the power to come and topple him down from his altitude by his vulgar threats; and never did a ringing of the bell at the gate of Nobbatop's villa announce an arrival without exciting a sort of fluttering sensation in the heart of the anxious and entirely disinterested lover, inasmuch as he feared it might be, intimately connected with his somewhat unfortunate affair with Kitty Catheral.

There is a fable about the cry of wolf—a
most apposite *sobriquet* for the " gent" in question,—wherein we are taught that frequent false
alarms engender indifference, when the brute
really arrives ; and, moreover, are there pro-
verbs as to pitchers going often to wells, and
not being broken ; still, as with Kitty—not
Kitty Catheral—but Kitty of Coleraine, the
event generally occurs at last.

One fine cold day, just as the party were
ready for a start, to take a healthful walk after
luncheon.—And here I must pause, to point out
this course of proceeding, as a practical mistake
in the autumn, inasmuch as the walk or drive
should be taken between breakfast and luncheon,
while the air is fresh, and the sun bright ;—
instead of which, luncheon lasting by the aid of
conversation from half-past one till half-past two,
the " lunchers" set out for their walks, rides, or
drives, just as the day is declining, and grope
their way home through cutting winds or drizzling
fogs in the dusk.

Where letters are to be answered, they may just as well be answered between the time of the return and the hour for dressing, as between breakfast and luncheon. This digression is intended to be advantageous to the health of numerous very delightful persons, who, without having so simple a notion put into their minds, might never think about it. In London, of course, no lady can order her carriage for a morning drive, until it is dusk; but in London people become the willing slaves of imperious fashion. In the country they may do as they like, although where the influence of what is called society is brought into operation even upon the invalids at watering-places, whose whole object one would presume to be health, the same observance of set rules is maintained. For instance: at Leamington nobody thinks in the winter of walking out of their houses till after their luncheons, somewhere about three o'clock. To be sure, many of them have been out to be drenched with the water, which is so satisfactorily and splendidly served out to them in the morning ; but as it is convenient for them to stay at home until a certain hour, all the rest of the people who drink no water, and do not get up early, think it necessary to stive themselves up till nearly dusk, before they take exercise, merely because " nobody goes out to walk till that time." What extraordinary minds some people must have, to submit to the operation of a general rule, and regulate their proceedings under · the dictum of a mob, for whose intellectual qualities, taking the herd individually, every one of their followers has the very meanest opinion.

Oh, independence !—not only pecuniary independence—but independence of mind and conduct — what a blessing art thou ! To be forced or induced to do this or that, or not to do either, because what one likes to do, happens not to be the fashion,—or what one does not like to do, is—seems a sort of slavery far worse than the fabled wretchedness of the negroes ;—to dine at eight, because it is the fashion, when one likes to dine at three;—to drive up and down Hyde Park in a dirty or a frosty evening—for evening it is—when one might enjoy a change of scenery and air, by varying the excursion. To be buttoned up twice a week for four hours in a hot cupboard, hung with scarlet fustian, in an ill-smelling place in the Haymarket, called the Opera House, to hear the same songs sung by the same people,—to see the same capers cut by the same jumpers, and to look at the same faces which one sees everyday everywhere else, seems one of the penalties paid—and at a high rate too by the sufferers—to fashion, hardly to be accounted for.

It is not that anybody will deny the beauty of the music, the skilfulness of the dancers, the talents of the performers, or the gaiety of the scene ; nor do we go the whole length of the saying, that people who haunt the opera resemble men in the pillory, and expose their heads while their ears are nailed. What to *us* makes the absurdity, is the regularity of attendance—the absolute necessity which exists in certain circles, of going to the opera on the Saturday, as the same people,. with a strange incongruity, recon- ileable, we presume, to their own principles and onsciences, feel for going to church on the Sun- day. A new opera—a new ballet—a new singer —a new dancer—the attractions of these we can understand; but the monotonous repetition of the same exhibitions night after night, and week after week, makes the *ridicule.* As to the conventional uses of the opera, nobody can doubt their advantages ' to society; and those would be pleaded by any lady of quality, who thought proper to defend the constancy of her visits.

Well, having made this preachment, we leave these cupboards and their curtains, and point the reader's attention to Mr. Peregrine Bunce, who was pacing up and down under the portico, waiting for the ladies, and who, while clapping his hands, partly in self-approbation of his success, and partly to make them warm, and who, just as he anticipated the friendly tap of summons from the fair hand of Maria Grayson, beheld approaching the house, an exceedingly shabby gig, drawn by a wretched looking horse, and containing as driver, the chief object of his horror, Mr. Hobsnob, exerting all his energies to urge on the lanky brute behind which he sat.

The apparition was a dreadful one to Peregrine—what was to be done ?—the vampyre had caught sight of his victim—he would be in front of the steps in one minute. Peregrine cast his eyes into the hall, and at the top of the staircase saw Maria Grayson with her foot on the highest step, in the first position for running down, to which exertion she had been excited by the idea, that the sound of carriage wheels announced visitors. It was impossible for Peregrine to know how the attorney might conduct himself, or what his first salutation might be ;— it was quite clear that to his lengthened stay at Nobbatop's, and his consequent inability to take up the I O U, as he had promised to do, was to be attributed the visitation; but all his calculations were upset, and his philosophy overthrown, when Maria, having reached the door one instant before Hobsnob, turned round to him, and said—

" La! what an odd looking little man!—what can he want here ?"

" How do you do, Mr. Bunce?" almost simultaneously with Miss Grayson's remark, said Mr. Hobsnob—fixing his eyes upon the unfortunate Peregrine's face, with an expression which at once conveyed the assurance, not only to the lover, but the lady, that he *had* some right to be there.

" How d'ye do ?—how dy'e do ?" said Peregrine, convinced that the only mode of proceeding, was by the way of conciliation.

" I see," said Hobsnob, " you are just going out—I won't detain you five minutes, if you will get somebody to hold my horse."

This request—to use a colloquial phrase—

"tickled the fancy" of the lively Maria amazingly —the necessity of standing at the head of a poor beast, which seemed to have exhausted all its energies to drag the man up to the place where his gig stood, was more than she could comprehend. However, with her accustomed good-nature, she gave a hearty tug at the bell by the door's side, and forthwith the sound like that of Roderick Dhu's horn, raised the vassals, and somebody was instantly ready to take charge of the "oss," as the attorney would have called it.

Hobsnob dismounted, and by his manner evidently implied that Peregrine could not go out upon his Philandering expedition, until he had favoured *him* with an audience. So Maria, who, although totally ignorant, even by suspicion, of the object of the vampyre's visit, begged Peregrine not to mind *them*, and to ask his acquaintance to do her uncle and aunt the favor of staying to dine, adding, that of course there would be a bed at his service.———" To dine !—

perchance to sleep !"——Peregrine " shuddered at
the gross idea !"——And after a consultation with
himself, which lasted only a few moments, he
resolved to let the ladies " walk on," and, having
settled his matters with the harpy, he would
follow them.

This was all very well ; but when Mrs. Nobbatop came out, be-furred and be-muffed for the
walk, and saw a stranger, nothing could restrain
her from offering the hospitality, for which her
husband was so remarkable, to any friend of
Peregrine's.   And there stood Peregrine in a
perfect horror——certain that the needy creature
would be too delighted to indulge his appetite
upon the slightest provocation, at anybody's
expense rather than his own; and certain, moreover, that the generous wine of his host after
dinner would, from his seldom being so gratified,
get into his head, and make him perhaps vul-
garly playful, and practically lively, or, in all
probability, induce an explanation of the cause
of his visit, and a detail of the whole affair of

his unfortunate, deluded client, Miss Katherine Catheral, and her faithless swain.

However, circumstances do sometimes occur, even in the worst positions, which are not to be anticipated. Hobsnob had hired his gig and horse—if he stayed, he would have had to pay for two days' usufruct ; and although he might have put that into his bill, in addition to the thirteen shillings and four-pence which he meant to charge, and in addition to the one day's chaise hire, which he of course also charged, he had a wife—a regular hair-comber, as they say in the country whence he came—a fine creature, who was master as well as mistress of the house, and who, if her husband did not perform his daily engagements precisely as they had been "programmed," proceeded to inflict a vengeance upon the poor creature, of which he often bore the marks upon his lily (orange lily) face. *He* dared not stay—and this *was* something to Bunce ; and so the ladies did walk on ; and a groom boy did sham standing by the wretched skeleton which had dragged him from Ditton to the villa, while Peregrine led his unwelcome visitor into the library.

" Well, Sir," said Hobsnob, " I presume you can account for my visit. Six days ago you gave me an I O U for four hundred pounds, with a promise that it should be taken up in *three* days. We have now waited a week, and—you will excuse me—we can wait no longer."

" But," said Peregrine, " don't you see, having prolonged my visit here, how could I go to town, to redeem the pledge I gave ?"

" I know nothing of visits, Sir," said Hobsnob. " I never make visits, nor do I receive visitors. I know that you promised to do a certain thing by a certain time, which thing you have not done. Now, Sir, that's the end of it."

" Well but ——"

" Aye, well but is extremely easy to say,"

replied the vampyre ;—" but *I* say that I must have the four hundred pounds.—Here is what you call your honourable obligation—fulfil it."

" I will," said Peregrine, " I give you my honour, the moment I go to town."

" Go to town," said the attorney, " why what's to hinder your going to town ? Five hours are all you want, there and back, and do the whole business in the interim — the rail-road ——."

" Yes," said Peregrine, " but *that* ——"

" If you don't like the rail-road, a pair of post horses will do it exactly as well," said the attorney, " or better, because you can drive straight to your broker's, or banker's, and get the affair settled off hand. I have done everything for you. I have three times stopped Miss Catheral from coming here. You really do not know, Mr. Bunce, what a valuable, and, as you will find in the end, what a disinterested friend, I have been to you."

" Then," said Bunce, " let me clearly under-

stand what your present particular and immediate object is."

" Merely to do that justice," said Hobsnob,
" and see it done to others, which I hope may
eventually be done to myself——in fact, Sir, in
four words, I want the money. The people of
whom I have already spoken to you are inces-
santly annoying my client—and not wishing her,
as I said before, to come down here ——"

" Ay, ay," said Peregrine, interrupting—
" I see—but really and truly, the difficulty with
me is, that without going to town I cannot
manage the matter."

" So you have already said,"replied the scum.
" Why then not go ?—I have pointed out the
facilities of conveyance ; or, if you prefer it, I
will avail myself of the kind invitation of the
lady of the house,—dine here, and sleep, and
drive you up in the morning. I have a clean
shirt front in my pocket-book, and, not showing
cuffs, I don't want dickies."

The latter part of the " gent's one" announce-

ment, Peregrine could understand, having himself fallen into the economical system of the
dirty dandy-school, of wearing clean " fronts,"
with " studs ;" but the idea of harbouring Hobsnob for the day, of subjecting himself to the
inflictions of his conversation—all the dread
that had filled his mind when Mrs. Nobbatop
had at first started the subject, came with
redoubled force into his imagination.

" No," said Peregrine, " I tell you what I
will do—I will be at your office on Thursday at
two—I will bring the money, and redeem the
bon—to this I pledge my honour."

" Why," said Hobsnob, shaking his head, and
looking as he always did,—" honour, Mr. Bunce,
is a certain something, of which I have no very
defined notion. I would in all cases where I
could, get it—prefer bail—that's *my* view of the
world—but, however, I suppose there would be
no objection to a feed of corn for the horse,
and a slight refreshment for myself. If you *are*

H 5

serious—for this time—and remember it *is* the last time—I will agree to your terms."

" Oh !" said Peregrine, " as to the horse—and yourself—why, of course, this is Liberty Hall—and you will be but too welcome." Saying which, and wishing him and his horse in a place to which horses are not generally supposed to go, he ordered some fresh luncheon to be put down, and directed Frank, the groom-boy, to take the horse round to the stables, and give him a feed.

Now, having done this, and gotten a reprieve as to the money until the Thursday, Peregrine Bunce, as the reader may imagine, walked himself off after the ladies : not a bit of it—he dared not trust the vampyre alone in the breakfast room, where the luncheon was served.——Not that, perhaps, Hobsnob would have stolen the forks or spoons, pocketed a salt-cellar, or carried off a mustard-pot ; but he was quite enough aware of his man—if man such a creature could

be called—to be assured that he would have
made friends with the servant, or servants, who
might have been in waiting upon him, to ferret
out the truth, which, from the very little he had
seen, he shrewdly (for these grubbers are exceedingly cunning in their low way) suspected
it to be, as to the real position of Peregrine
Bunce in the Nobbatop establishment. Therefore, with a much more sensitive regard for his
own interests, than for the portable plate of his
munificent host, Peregrine resolved on giving
his odious visitor no chance of being, as they
say, left to himself.

The walk was, of course, abandoned—*that* did
not so much signify—but as the vampyre, who
lived at home much as did the respectable and
universally lamented Mr. Elwes, or the never-
to-be-sufficiently regretted Mr. Dancer, of Har-
row-weald, who, when the late Marquis of
Abercorn sent him some turtle, warmed it for
dinner by putting it between two pewter-plates
in his bed, and lying upon it until it was hot

enough to be eaten,——was most assiduous in his attentions to the *matériel* which had been placed before him; and as it began about the same time to snow slightly, the agonies of Peregrine lest the promenaders should return before he had finished his operations, coupled with the positive certainty, that if it set in for snow in any serious degree, his kind hostess would not permit his friend to turn out under any circumstances, kept him in a state of nervousness which nobody who has not felt something a little like it, can possibly understand.

Every huge bit of meat which the vampyre threw in from the deep cavern of a vast Strasbourg pie, was watched by Peregrine with an anxiety wholly indescribable——that any *one* of the masses should have terminated his existence, would have been to Peregrine a much smaller calamity, than the continuance of his persevering assiduity in successfully swallowing it. He walked to the window——looked at the snow—— then, by way of being civil, and of cheering his

own spirits, took a glass of wine with his unwelcome companion.——Deuce a bit did Hobsnob
seem inclined to move. ·

" Nice place this," said he, helping himself to
a bumper of Madeira, and just drawing away
his chair from the table, as much as to express
practically, " I can't eat any more."——" You are
fortune's favourite, Mr. B."

" I am exceedingly happy," said Peregrine,
" to be so well received here ; and I rather
thank you for your call to-day, for it reminds
me, that a man ought never to wear out a friend's
hospitality."

" Ay, ay," said the vampyre, warmed with
the wine, " I guess how it is——I have said so——
mum——all will be right——only, for your own sake,
don't fail Thursday——I assure you, my great
interest is in *you*."

" Well, then," said Peregrine, " accept my
thanks now."

" I declare to you," said Hobsnob, " as I am
an honest man, nothing but my working would

have saved you from exposure ; as I say, Mr. Bunce, the true spirit of law is equity.   I am, at one and the same time, for and against you. —Nothing like it, Sir.   I do all I can for Kitty—all I can for *you ;*—and it is my way of working.   Some low people, Mr. Bunce, may think I do it to get costs, and all that, on both sides ; but such folks know but little of *me*, Sir.   There's a ruling power above ; and in all I have done through life, I have laboured for the best."

Peregrine seeing that the " gent. one" was getting *raather* forward in his course of imbibition, gently inquired whether he should order his gig round.

" To be sure," said Hobsnob, filling another glass of Madeira.   " Order it round, or order it square—I'm all for fun—you do not know what a droll dog I am, when I'm what Mrs. Hobsnob calls 'cocky.'—Ha! ha ! ha !—Here, come, let us drink one glass together, eh ?"

" Order Mr. Hobsnob's gig to the door,"

said Peregrine Bunce to a servant who answered
the bell.

" Let us—I say, Mr. Bunce, let us drink one
glass together," stammered out the attorney,
" may we never meet, or part, worse friends
than we are now, eh ?"—And there were tears in
the eyes of the hyena.

The present aspect of affairs was to Peregrine's mind almost worse than the past. The
hypocritical humbug, elated by Nobbatop's good
wine, now turned to be facetious, and became
proportionately more disgusting to Peregrine,
inasmuch as it was clear that one thing or the
other must be false. The pious-looking, demure
character, which Hobsnob had hitherto affected,
must have been an assumption ; or the lively
hilarity and playfulness which he now exhibited,
must be an imposition. However, as soon as
the gig was announced, Peregrine, having
pledged his honour to see him in the dirty hole
which he called his chambers, hurried him out
of the house, caring, perhaps, as little as any

man ever did for the safety of another in a
drunken drive, qualifying the indifference of his
feelings upon two strong points—one, that such
a nag never could run away with anybody, and
the other, that such an attorney could, by no
possibility, die of a broken neck—from a one
horse chaise.

The sight of the departing raff, before the
return of the ladies, almost outweighed the per-
turbation which Peregrine had felt when he arrived, before their leaving the house. However,
he found, that having pledged himself, he had but
the one alternative left—he must go to town on
the Thursday, and do that which he had been
cajoled, persuaded, or threatened into, by his
legal opponent—professing himself at the same
time to be his friend ; and so, Peregrine having
witnessed the entire evanishment of his Snar-
lywow, made a fresh start, to endeavour to
intercept the ladies on their return.

All people in country-houses have what may
be called their peculiar haunts, and particular

routes; and so, by a little attention—and it was
not a little attention that Peregrine paid to such
details—he tracked and caught the pedestrian
party on their return, and was repaid for his
pleasing pain, by finding Maria Grayson, his
companion, as he walked down from Grimbledon-
hill, which it was considered healthy to mount
now and then; the worry of the ascent being
inconceivable to anybody but the medical man
who recommended it as wholesome, which,
coupled with the slippery descent, reduced the
beautiful Maria precisely to the state in which
the arm of a man for whom a young lady has,
at least, a warm esteem, becomes a remarkably
agreeable support.

The unbounded kindness of Mrs. Nobbatop
was sadly outraged by Peregrine's account of
Mr. Hobsnob's departure—why didn't he stay?
Mr. Nobbatop would have been so glad of his
company, and lawyers—for Peregrine had this
time mentioned his friend's profession—were
in general so very agreeable—the poor lady not

knowing or comprehending, that there are not in creation two beings so completely opposite to each other in manners, character, or attributes, as the high-minded, gentlemanly practitioner, and the paltry pettifogger, of which class Hobsnob was, perhaps, the most striking example. However, as he was gone, Peregrine cared little more than to express his friend's great regret at being obliged to return to town on business, and to insinuate, that his visit had been occasioned by the extraordinary anxiety of his uncle Oliver, to see that a certain property which he possessed in Gloucestershire, in right of his mother, should be well looked after. And so Peregrine laughed, and joked—and so Maria was pleased—and so they all came back, to warm themselves round the fire before they parted to dress for dinner, the ladies falling into the wise and agreeable custom of taking a cup of tea in their dressing-rooms before they commenced that operation.

Nobbatop arrived, as usual, bringing with

him not only his son, but a friend, an exceedingly melancholy gentleman, who spoke monosyllabically, but who was supposed to be one of the greatest capitalists in the country. He assented or dissented merely by " yeas " and " nays," and was to Maria an object, not of hatred, because she cared too little about him to hate him, but of ridicule ; and her great difficulty, when he visited them, which he occasionally did, was to constrain her propensity for imitating his pertinent but uninteresting brevities. He was somehow intimately connected with the concerns of the firm, and was always treated *en grand Seigneur*, upon the occasion of his becoming an inmate of the villa.

The happy family circle, however, surrounded the hospitable board, Mr. Towsey being the only out-of-door visitor ; and nothing could be more agreeable. Peregrine having perfectly recovered from the visitation of the vampyre, and Nobbatop being more than usually eloquent upon the subjects of which he was really master,

the conversation went about like a foot-ball.
Mr. Saxby Mumps, the man of much money,
but few words, sending it on by his monosyllabic kicks, with the greatest effect.

Never, perhaps, were exhibited, in juxta-
position, two persons, engaged in similar pursuits, more diametrically opposed to each other
in manner or character, than this very Mr.
Saxby Mumps and Mr. Jeremiah Nobbatop.
The warm, ardent, sanguine, speculative mind of
Nobbatop, developing itself in glowing descrip-
tions of the various great operations in which
he was concerned, formed the most extraordinary, and, it must be admitted, agreeable
contrast to the cold, brief, and melancholy
observations of his friend, who never failed, let
what might be the question, to throw in a gloomy
doubt of its probable advantage or success.

Whether it was on the admitted principle,
that people in this world are always pleased with
those who are as unlike themselves in disposition and character as possible, or for any other

more cogent reason, it is an undoubted fact, that whenever Nobbatop wanted advice—as it should seem — Mr. Saxby Mumps appeared at the villa, and, upon the present occasion, it seeming to Towsey and Peregrine, that the two Nobbatops and their guest, wished to talk over something, of doubtless great importance to themselves, they betook themselves to the drawing-room.

And was not this the opportunity for " cornerizing" Maria ?—Was not this the proper moment for alluding to her cousin's approaching marriage, Surely, if Towsey would but occupy the attention of Mrs. Nobbatop, this *would* be the time. If Towsey had been bribed, he could not have done better what Peregrine desired, for not only did he occupy the attention of the matron, but challenged her to a game of billiards, in the which " mace-wise," she was a proficient.

Just imagine Peregrine, with the opportunity (if, as the country maids say, he could spell it,

and put it together,) once more in the first
position for " popping,"—not pointedly, personally, and particularly—but, for putting into
execution his projected scheme of making a sort
of hypothetical affair of it, in its present stage,
by referring to George Nobbatop's approaching
happiness with his affectionate Miss Screecher.
Just imagine it—alone, by the side of his Maria
on a sofa—the men engaged in their mercantile
speculations in the dining room, and his friend
and the lady of the house at billiards, a game of
which the noise of knocking the balls about,
gives evidence of its progress, and the consequent
security from any immediate interruption by the
players—imagine this, and doubt for a moment
the course that Peregrine, not badly " cham-
pagned up" for the purpose, would pursue.

Peregrine certainly never had been so well
received upon any of his predatory excursions,
as by Miss Grayson, for the best of all possible
reasons, with which the reader is already acquainted—namely, that she really *did* like him ;

and so, while she was affecting to read, or do some nonsensical work, or something of the kind, our friend Perry " screwed his courage to the sticking place," and began :—

" What a happy creature," said Peregrine, turning over the leaves of a book which lay amongst a heap of others on the table before him—" What a happy creature your cousin George must be—so near the realization of all his hopes and wishes."

" Yes," said Maria, " I dare say he *is*,"— which she said in a tone which led Mr. Peregrine Bunce to think that Miss Grayson's admiration of the bride elect was not altogether unqualified.

" It must be," said Peregrine, " something more delightful than those who have never felt it can even imagine, to find one's affections reciprocated—and—to be conscious that one is loved."

" I dare say," said Maria Grayson, " it must be very agreeable," and she fidgetted about a

little, as if she suspected, or rather expected,
a more serious turn in the dialogue.

" How," said Peregrine,—" how is it possible
that *he*, with all the advantages of your society
—a constant association with you—and an intimate knowledge of all your charms aud excellence—could have looked from home for a———."

" Ah," said Maria, " there it is—there is a
proverb which my uncle often uses, ' that a man
is never a prophet in his own country.' So,
I suppose all my perfections, which, as you
say, are so very remarkable, were entirely lost
upon George."

" Lost indeed," said Peregrine; "but perhaps,
Miss Grayson, the fault is yours;—you, who
seem to me to be omnipotent in conquest, may
have repelled—repulsed him—and so ———."

" No, no," said Maria, " to tell you the truth,
we have been going on living and living more
like brother and sister, than cousins; and I
don't think that a thought of any other kind
of affection ever entered either of our heads;

besides, I don't believe that George ;—that is, I ——— "

And here Maria became a little confused— Peregrine saw his advantage.

" What do you *not* believe ?" said Peregrine, placing himself in an attitude which indicated his desire to take her hand.

" Why," said Maria, " I do not exactly know what I do *not* believe. What I do believe is, that we had better go into the billiard room, and see after my aunt's game. They will want somebody to mark for them."

And so down went the book, up jumped Maria Grayson, and away she ran ; Peregrine after her, satisfied, as indeed under the circumstances he seemed justified in being, that he *was* settled at last ; in fact, no man of the world could for a moment doubt the real state of the case. To be sure, when they *were* in the billiard-room, and Maria, with all the calm collectedness which ladies at all times, and under all trying circumstances, have at command, began to score

the game, with an interest in the play so beau-
tifully acted, that anybody who did not know
the truth, must have believed it genuine ; Bunce
riveted his eyes upon her with a look of the
deepest and most intense interest.   He beheld
in that dear, unaffected, accomplished, yet un-
pretending girl, a store of happiness exceed-
ing anything that ever, in his most sanguine
days, he had expected to obtain.   Maria saw
his look.   She understood — appreciated it—
approved—reciprocated it—and that, too, just
at the moment that Mr. Towsey was proclaimed
the loser of a love game.

Any attempt to describe the state of Peregrine's sensations at the moment would be hope-
less.   All he could do to assure himself of the
reality of the bright vision which had dazzled
his sight, and filled his whole mind with rapture, was to try whether a second glance would
be equally well received.   However, rallying his
energies, he crossed the room to the fire-place,
over which the marking tables were fixed, and

before which the fair marker stood, and, affecting some doubt as to her honesty in scoring, contrived to touch her fair hand, which was neither angrily nor scornfully withdrawn. That settled it.

Only think for a moment how Peregrine at *that* moment felt. He was thrown into a reverie—a waking or rather wakeful dream. His eyes again rested on her—his heart beat—nay, even his limbs trembled. There could be no longer a doubt —— "

At that period entered the billiard-room, Nobbatop, Saxby Mumps, and George, who, having discussed their dry business over sundry bottles, now felt it necessary to dissipate in the gayer circles of the establishment. Mr. Saxby Mumps, whose face looked like the moon in a mist, with a halo of white hair, complimented Mrs. Nobbatop upon her skill at billiards.

" Yes," said she, " I like playing billiards; not so much for the game itself, but as it induces exercise."

" Good," said Mumps.

" Don't *you* play ?" said the lady, laying down
the mace with the air of a shepherdess resigning
her crook.

" No," said Mumps.

" What, do you dislike billiards?" said Maria.

" No," said Mumps.

" And yet," said Maria, " you don't play."

" No," said Mumps, gliding off to a corner of
the room, to whisper some other monosyllables
into Nobbatop's ear.

" Come, George," said Peregrine, " a game ?"

" With all my heart," said George.

And so the ball was pointed, and the play
begun ; but where were Peregrine's eyes?——
What were the kisses and misses of the game
to the object of his idolatry ? She marked—
and probably re-marked the success of her last
encouraging glance ; not being at all aware of
the appositeness of her observation touching
Peregrine's peculiarities of performance, when
she observed, " that he seldom made a losing
hazard, but always played for the pocket."

Had Dumbledore been there, he would have made some horrid joke ; and if Uncle Noll had been of the party, he would have sported something worse, inasmuch as it would have been a truism relative to his hopeful nephew's speculative pursuits, which, it must be owned, now appeared to be drawing to an exceedingly happy conclusion.

" My love," said Mr. Nobbatop, as the evening wore on, or rather wore out—" Mr. Mumps, George, and myself, must start before breakfast in the morning."

" What !" said Mrs. Nobbatop, " nothing on your stomach ?—Oh, no—why—"

" I don't mean *that*, dear," said the great capitalist, " I mean before *your* breakfast time ; —it is of the very greatest importance that we should get our letters at the earliest possible moment to-morrow."

" Well but surely," said Mrs. Nobbatop, " you will breakfast before you go—what matters the hour ?"

" My love," said the fond husband, " manage
that as you please. Give Mrs. Ferrett her
orders ;—all I mean to say is, that we must be
away from this by seven."

" Seven, love," exclaimed the lady, with a
look of horror, " why it's dark at seven."

" We," said Nobbatop, " who are men of
business and of circumstances, care little about
day or night; we must be off ;—what say you,
Mr. Mumps ?"

" Poz !" said Mr. Mumps.

" Of course," said the lady of the house, " it
is my duty to obey—so I will take care that
everything shall be ready in time."

" Or," said George, playfully, " what do you
think, my dear mother, if we made a night of it,
and sat up till the time came."

" No," said Mumps, shaking his head, in
order to save himself the trouble of repeating
the monosyllabic negative.

" Oh, all shall be ready," said the dear kind
hostess, " only I could not think of letting Mr.

N. go out in the morning, this weather, without something on his stomach, for the world."

Peregrine, who had been making his play rather effectively with Maria at the end of the billiard-table, teaching her to spin the ball with her fingers, and other manœuvres connected with the game, had ears sufficiently long to catch enough of the conversation which was passing in the divan, to ascertain that he,— " forced by duty," (although " racked by love,") to go to town himself in the morning, had no chance of a place in Nobbatop's carriage. As a set-off to this defeat, he would, however, have the opportunity of further ingratiating himself, during the regular breakfast and the two or three following hours, then riding over to Ditton, and thence posting to town ; or perhaps, if he found it not unpleasant, taking the whole distance on horseback. However, he thought it right to intimate the necessity of his departure, and—at least, his temporary—absence for a couple of days.

" I am sorry," said Peregrine, advancing to

I 4

the main body of the party, Maria having thought it right to abandon her teacher, whose anxiety for her advancement in the "noble game,"she fancied might attract more notice than was quite desirable—"that I must also leave you to-morrow, Mrs. Nobbatop—it *is*, I admit, to me a very painful separation, but———"

"Why," said the benevolent lady, "where are *you* going?—what can you have to do?—you are not like my husband and son, tied, as I say, to their desks."

"No," said Peregrine, "but I mentioned to you, yesterday, the anxiety of my kind uncle to secure my right to a little property, which I have in Gloucestershire, and I feel it a duty to so kind a relation—indeed the nearest relation I have in the world—not to seem to neglect his wishes, even though the object, as far as I myself am concerned, may not be of any very great importance."

"But," said Mrs. Nobbatop, "you will come back to us?"

" You are too kind," said Peregrine, bowing;
" *I* shall be too happy."

" Well then," said Maria, who returned from
her hunt after nothing in the adjoining room,
" you will be our only cavalier at breakfast.—
You, Mr. Towsey —— ?"

" Oh I," said Towsey, " am off directly. I
have ordered my carriage at ten, and must not
hope to see you to-morrow."

In fact, Mr. Towsey, who was a most patient
lover, had seen quite enough that evening to
satisfy himself of the perfect inefficacy of any
future efforts of *his*, towards gaining the heart
of Miss Grayson, and had resolved, if he ever
did again visit the villa, for the sake of the
exceedingly agreeable society, and the remarkably good dinners, he would never attempt any
further progress in his siege of the heart of the
wealthy Nobbatop's adopted daughter.

Time wore on—flew, as Peregrine thought—
the supper, never missed at Nobbatop's, was announced—eaten or looked at—the *life-refreshing*

liquors, were imbibed——adieux were reciprocated
——candles were lighted——the ladies evanished——
the men just took *one* glass more, which, although it might be low and vulgar, was the way
of the house.   Mumps sipped, and said nothing.
Nobbatop drank little, but talked much—was
eloquent upon bonds, and loans, and other matters, of which Peregrine was not, in the slightest
degree, cognizant ; nor if he *had* been, could he
have commanded his thoughts to such subjects,
while his whole heart and mind were concentred
in Maria.   So, when the clock struck twelve,
the party separated ; and Peregrine, having promised to return on the second day after his
departure from Slambury, the various members
of the family retired to rest.

CHAPTER XVI.

PEREGRINE was not a genuine, true-hearted, generous person, as we too well know. The success he had evidently met with in his career with Maria, would, in a high-minded, ardent, and ingenuous lover, have kept him awake during the night which followed, what we may really call, the unequivocal admission of her feelings towards him. He would have tossed and tumbled in his bed, restless and sleepless, and anxious for the coming day, to renew that happy interchange of affection which had so cheered and charmed him when they parted; and would, with all the ardour of a sanguine mind, have pictured in his waking thoughts

I 6

that which, had he slept, would have influenced his dreams—the happiness in store for him when she should be really his. A thousand various schemes of domestic happiness would have presented themselves to his imagination ; and he would have risen with the lark to seek his loved one at the earliest moment at which she was stirring.

No—these sweet genuine feelings of devotion, anxious beyond all other objects for the security, the comfort, the heart-welcome of the dear, tender, affectionate being, who had smiled upon him, nay, who had virtually accepted him, disturbed not the repose of Mr. Peregrine Bunce. He rolled himself up in the cold sheets, which his crawling blood had not power to warm, and began to inquire, and calculate, and consider, how the forty thousand pounds Maria was to have, were invested. The consent of Nobbatop he did not fear to gain ; but then, might not he, as the fortune was to come from himself, impose some conditions? Oh that

word !—The lover who talks of conditions—
who hesitates — who pauses — who calculates !
But why write a word upon the subject ?—We
all know `Mr. Peregrine Bunce pretty well by
this time.

Correct as clockwork, Mr. Nobbatop, senior,
Mr. Nobbatop, jun. and Mr. Saxby Mumps,
congregated round the candle-lighted breakfast-
table in the morning, and quitted Slambury,
as ordered and ordained, by seven o'clock ; the
great object being to receive the earliest intelligence of something that was going to happen
somewhere in Europe, Asia, Africa, or America,
but in which, excepting themselves and some
other set of people, who were trying, as the sailors
say, to " get to windward of them," nobody upon
the face of the earth—at least British earth—
was in the slightest degree either concerned or
interested.

After a more than usually careful toilette,
Mr. Peregrine Bunce proceeded towards the
breakfast-room, having told his valet-groom to

have his horses ready at eleven, dreading, as he
did, another warning from Hobsnob, and sincerely wishing him in advance, in that place to
which both in right of his professional pursuits
and private character, he was eventually doomed
and destined.

Maria's morning manner was in just accord-
ance with her previous evening kindness—proportionably less ardent, inasmuch as morning is
not, as Moore says, the genial hour for burning ;
but it was all that Peregrine could wish, and
infinitely more than he could have hoped.   The
bright eyes that the night before had sparkled
with pleasure, while she listened to his conversation, now rested with a mild and gentle
radiance on his countenance, and the thrice
repeated inquiry, whether he really *must* go, was
made with a quiet, but evidently unaffected,
earnestness, which seemed only mitigated by the
equally earnest declaration of his resolution to
return " the day after to-morrow."

Mrs. Nobbatop, who could not bear what is

called a break-up of a snug little party, suggested fifty plans for getting all the business he had to do in town, transacted for him. He would be so missed—and dear Mr. Nobbatop, whose mind was all day harassed by important occupations, was so delighted with his society, and so on—little suspecting the nature of the affair to which Mr. Peregrine Bunce's attention had been so peremptorily attracted.

This kind lady's persuasions and entreaties, however, were vain ; and after luncheon, (for, in spite of all remonstrances, they would not permit him to start before,) Peregrine took his departure from Slambury, receiving in return for the cordial shake of her hand, a reciprocal pressure from that of Maria, which thrilled through his heart, beating as it did at the moment with indescribable delight at having secured forty or fifty thousand pounds, with the enjoyment, probably for many years to come, of such an establishment as that, which *malgré lui* he was compelled temporarily to quit, but to which he meant, having disposed of his little diffi-culties *in re* Catheral, to return as speedily as possible.

One condition, however, was positively insisted upon: namely, that he *must* be the bearer of an invitation to his uncle. Maria seemed extremely earnest in pressing this, and gave at least a dozen reasons why Mr. Oliver Bunce would be so happy and comfortable at Slambury, and the pleasure her uncle would feel in his society. Mrs. Nobbatop seconded all these solicitations and suggestions, because she saw Maria's anxiety on the point ; an anxiety which arose out of the natural solicitude to become acquainted with so important a branch of a family, with which it seems she had almost made up her mind to become shortly connected.

It was impossible for Peregrine to do anything but express his gratitude for their attentions, and, of course, promise to convey their kind welcome to the old gentleman; hinting, however, that he did not think he would venture upon a new engagement, as the year was closing, and he made a point to be at his own home at Christmas. In fact, Peregrine was not at all anxious that Noll should come to Slambury until he had made his " *assurance* doubly sure," and perfectly secured his prize ; for up to the present moment, nothing had been said to prevent Maria's rejection of him, if unfortunately she, or her uncle, or her aunt, or her cousin, should take a dislike to Noll. To such a man as Dumbledore, Peregrine had been perfectly safe in introducing him ; but even *there* he kept him upon thorns as long as the short visit lasted : here the matter was totally different, and the subject required consideration ; so he contented himself by promising to use all his eloquence to induce his worthy relative to accept their kind invitation ; and so professing, he made preparations for his departure.

And then, to see how Mrs. Nobbatop took care of him—how she would insist upon his having an extra handkerchief round his throat—and

muffatees on his wrists, and entreating him to be
sure, if he should get wet on his journey, to change
his clothes immediately on his arrival at home.

Poor Mrs. Nobbatop!——Home, Peregrine had
none——nor was it until he had ridden some six
or seven miles that it struck him, that, as all
the mischief of the discovery of his residence in
town by Kitty had been done ; and as he had
been driven into making up his mind to settle
that affair, he might as well go straight back to
his old lodgings, whither his worthy man Tim
could, with the greatest facility, re-transport his
master's trunks, and where, supposing his rooms
were not let, he might locate himself until he
became a Benedick.

Accordingly, when he made a brief halt at
Richmond, to give his favourite bay a few
minutes' rest, (having resolved upon riding to
town,) he imparted to Tim his intention of
going straight back to the " place whence he
came," which announcement seemed to Tim
somewhat needless, inasmuch as *he* was not aware

of any reason why a gentleman leaving his
lodgings for a country excursion, should *not*
return to them. This did not at the moment
strike Peregrine, whose whole mind was occupied in the concoction of sinister designs, and
the contrivance of underhand manœuvres ; and
who thought that Tim, with all his readiness of
comprehension and inquisitiveness of disposition,
was, in fact, in full possession of the real cause
of his sudden abdication.

This not being the case, the return to the
lodgings was duly effected. They were still
vacant, and the landlord and landlady quite
glad to see Peregrine back again. Tim was
despatched to put up the horses in the place,
where his heart was already installed, and if he
were not quite so soon back from the errand,
the reader will recollect that his Dulcinea dwelt
over the stables, and that his affection for her
might be well pleaded as an excuse for any little
delay.

Peregrine cared nothing for the tardiness of

his return. He had given him orders to get back
the trunks which he so short a time before had
directed him to remove, and, in fact, to replace
him in his old apartments : all which operations
could be performed while he himself went to
fulfil his engagement with Mr. Hobsnob—an
engagement which, in every sense of the word,
was most disagreeable to him ; and not the less
so, because, upon calculating and " totting up,"
it did not clearly appear to him, that he had
anything in the way of ready cash amounting to
a sufficient sum to meet the I O U which he
had given.

He knew not the individual character of Mr.
Hobsnob, but he knew the generic merits of his
class of practitioners too well to doubt for a moment that he would do anything and everything
to annoy him on the part of Miss Catheral, (who,
in all probability, had attracted his particular
attention, for particular reasons, although, as has
been already said, the creature had a wife and
family of his own,) to leave, just at this critical

juncture, a chance of an exposure which might overthrow all his brightest expectations; or, knowing what we do of Miss Grayson's real feelings, *we* may say, splendid certainties.

Therefore did Peregrine Bunce repair to his banker's book—find himself below the mark, in the way of balance; but, with his prospects, the securities he possessed, and all the rest of it, no difficulty could possibly occur, on account of so small a sum, and Peregrine proceeded to the dirty den of the extortioner with four nice new one hundred pound notes, looking by far too clean and delicate, to be pawed by such hands as Hobsnob's.

In his way from his banker's to the harpy, he thought it right, and prudent, and proper, to favour his uncle with a call at the Tavistock Hotel,—the large, wild, rambling house or houses, where Noll, in company with hundreds of other worthy and respectable people, had been, as we already know, for several years, domesticated when in town.

As a proof of the vastitude of the affairs connected with London society, in its different classes and degrees, and of the possibility of utter seclusion in the midst of all its various pursuits, it is a fact on record, that one inhabitant of that popular and (to a great extent) convenient hotel, lived in it for several years unknown by any other designation than that of the number of the room which he occupied. And that in another instance of a similar nature, but where the inmate had not been so long domiciled' there, a gentleman having destroyed himself in a fit of insanity, the chambermaid, to whom the care of his apartment was confided, rushed into the bar with a countenance full of horror, and exclaimed to the landlord, " What do you think, Sir ?——Number 37 has shot himself !"

At this hotel Peregrine Bunce called——his uncle was from home ; Peregrine left word that he would call again, and proceeded to the miserable chambers, as Hobsnob called a dirty hole on a third floor of the dirtiest inn—nominally of court—in London. *He* was not from home—not he—he sat like a spider—(with many companions about the apartment,) spinning his six and eight-penny meshes; and the only thing that ever cheered up his death-like countenance was a rap at the door, which announced the approach of a victim, just as a regular Aranea twiddles and twitches his feelers when a stray fly merely hits upon a filament of his dirt constructed web.

As a striking evidence of the total change of manners, and the relative positions and conditions of men during the last two hundred years, the following account of what an attorney in *his* day was, from the pen of the right reverend and right learned author of " Microcosmography," may not be uninteresting, although, it is probable, well enough known :—

" An attorney's ancient beginning," says the Bishop, " was a blue coat ;—since a livery, and his hatching under a lawyer ; whence, though but pen-feathered, he hath now nested for himself, and with his hoarded pence, purchased an office. Two desks, and a quire of paper, set him up, where he now sits in state for all comers. We can call him no author, yet he writes very much, and with the infamy of the court is maintained in his libels. He has some smatch of a scholar, and yet uses Latin very hardly; and lest it should accuse him, cuts it off in the midst, and will not let it speak out. He is, contrary to great men, maintained by his followers, that is, his poor country clients that worship him more than their landlord, and, be they never such churls, he looks for their courtesy. He first racks them soundly himself, and then delivers them to the lawyer for execution. His looks are very solicitous, importing much haste and dispatch ; he is never without his hands full of business, that is, of paper. His skin becomes at last as dry as his parchment, and his face as intricate as the most winding cause. He talks statutes as fiercely as if he had mooted seven years in the inns of court ;

where all his skill is stuck in his girdle, or in his office-window. Strife and wrangling have made him rich, and he is thankful to his bene-factors, and nourishes it. If he live in a country village, he makes all his neighbours good sub-jects ; for there shall be nothing done but what there is law for. His business gives him not leave to think of his conscience ; and when the time or term of his life is going out, for dooms-day he is secure ; for he hopes he has a trick to reverse judgment."

The Bishop's lively description, taken with a just and proper allowance for the difference of manners and habits, is curious. However, Pe-regrine was not prejudiced in his intercourse with Hobsnob by any such " foregone con-clusions," but, instinctively and inherently mean and shuffling as he was himself, he almost shuddered as he gave a rat-tat with the little brass knocker, on the inner door of the vam-pyre's rooms, who, expecting a dupe, did not on that day sport oak.

The dialogue between Peregrine and the harpy was short and not sweet. The look of the lawyer—the tone of his voice—the hypocritical seriousness of a creature who was a regular wag and a practical joker amongst his fellows in society—the interest which he affected to take in Katherine—the smell of the place in which he lived—the chilly damp of it—the whole combination of circumstances — hurried Peregrine to the conclusion of the interview, at which it arrived when he handed over to the vampyre the four hundred pounds, as promised, and received a receipt in full of all demands from him on the part of his client, Miss Katherine Catheral, together with the I O U which, of course, she had never seen.

" Would you," said Hobsnob, " like to see her ?—after so intimate an acquaintance, perhaps some feeling of regard may remain."

" No," said Peregrine, " certainly not. I do not consider that I have been fairly treated in this business. To be sure, our meeting at

Brighton was wholly unexpected, and as it turned out, disastrous; but no, tell her that I shall always wish her well, in spite of what I think has been her misconduct; and so, Sir, I wish you a good morning."

Hobsnob rose from a dirty black leathern chair, through the much worn seat of which a tuft of grizzly horse-hair protruded, and rang a bell which was cracked, and upon which the twisted and rusty wire refused to act; wherefore it did not awaken a wretched scrub, son of a neighbouring shoe-black, who earned two shillings a week from Hobsnob for sitting on a high stool in the outer room of the two, and acting clerk upon any day whenever any body was expected to call upon business. Hobsnob, however, ushered Peregrine out; having done which he gave the boy a waking kick, and then retired to his own den, where, looking over his arrangement of the affairs of Miss Catheral, he came to the conclusion, that having compromised with her creditors for about seven shillings in the pound, one hundred pounds would settle *them*, while by handing her over another hundred, (short his bill, which amounted to forty-eight, ten, and six,) he should behave nobly, and pocket the other two hundred, beyond what he considered his legitimate costs, as a just and proper remuneration for having relieved his fair client from all further responsibility, and displayed sufficient generosity on the part of Peregrine, to secure him from any further applications from " the damsel all forlorn," this being even a better bargain for her, than we had anticipated.

If the attorney felt delighted with his skill, and its success, Peregrine, as he paced the streets towards Covent Garden, to re-visit his uncle's domicile, was equally satisfied ; he had settled *that* affair—he was safe. Maria Grayson was his own, and after all, what *were* four hundred pounds in such a case, when everything was taken into consideration.

Uncle Noll had not returned when Peregrine

called again at the Tavistock, but he saw there
the faithful Limpus, and learned from him that
he did not expect his master home till late in
the evening, for that he was gone to dine somewhere out of town, and more than that, from
something he had said when he set forth, it
appeared highly probable to Limpus, that he
might not even return to sleep.

This was a kind of damper to Peregrine, whose
great object was always to enlighten his uncle
upon any point which he had successfully achieved.
However, the disappointment was nothing but a
delay of gratification, and therefore he left word
with the trusty servant, that he would call at
four o'clock the next day, and hoped to have
the pleasure of dining with his uncle somewhere
—there being no dinners at the Tavistock—
inasmuch as the morning after the next, he
must return to Slambury Park—which *he* always
called Nobbatop's place, although Nobbatop
himself never did—and therefore he trusted his
" dear uncle " would be disengaged. To this

affectionate message he added the information, that he had returned to his old lodgings, and that if his uncle preferred any other arrangement, or had any other proposition to make, if he sent him a note, his wishes should be obeyed in every particular.

How Uncle Noll passed his evening, or how his nephew Peregrine passed *his*, history does not inform us ; but this we know, that about one o'clock the next day, Peregrine received a note from Noll, telling him he should be glad to see him at his hotel about half-past five, and there they could settle some plan for the disposal of themselves for the rest of the afternoon.

It has been already noticed, that from the scantiness of his acquaintance, and as it seemed, his total want of friends of his own age and standing, Peregrine had nobody in the world to sympathize with him in his grief, or rejoice with him in his happiness.   It was this fact which filled him with anxiety for the arrival of the

hour at which he might open his heart and
mind to his nearest relation, and the postpone-
ment of the time of their meeting for an hour
and a half beyond that which he had suggested,
vexed him ; so high were his spirits, and so
ardent was his enthusiasm.

Peregrine, when he left " Slambury Park,"
had made something like a half promise to write
a few lines to say how he got to town, and what
his uncle had said in answer to the invitation
which Mrs. Nobbatop had sent him, and, in
fact, to say a great many of the agreeable
nothingnesses, of which such notes are ordinarily
composed.

Now Peregrine was a disciple of that prudential school, the leading doctrine of which is,
" never to write a letter to a woman, and never
to destroy a letter which a woman has written to
you ;" and although in the present case, nothing
could come of his writing anything he pleased,
he nevertheless resolved if he *did* write, to
write to Mrs. Nobbatop.——Maria might think

it presumptuous, if he wrote to *her ;* besides, he could more successfully write *at* her in the letter to her aunt, than he could *to* her in a letter to herself ; whereupon, after mature deliberation, he penned the following :—

" ———— *Street,*

" —— 1840.

" MY DEAR MADAM,

" I arrived safe and sound at my old residence, and which, till I had tasted the charms of Slambury, I used to fancy exceedingly agreeable, and even lively ; but now—and it is your fault—every thing seems dull, and dreary, and dismal ; and I wonder how I could have formed so false an estimate of its advantages.

" I really have no words to thank you for the hospitality and kindness which I have received from you and Mr. Nobbatop, nor the pleasureable hours which I have passed in the delightful society of your family circle. Pray tell Miss

Grayson, that the first thing I did on reaching town was to send to buy those two beautiful songs which she sang so delightfully the night before last, which seems an age ago. However, thanks to your kindness, my banishment will not be of long duration.

" I have not yet seen my uncle, upon whom I called twice yesterday, but I have heard from him to-day, and am to dine with him this evening, when I shall deliver your kind message to him. I wish he may be able to avail himself of your friendly offer, for I should very much like to present him to you, as a most worthy specimen of an old English gentleman.

" I look forward with the deepest anxiety to the hour when I am permitted to return to your Paradise ; and if I do not succeed in bringing my uncle with me, I trust very soon to have the privilege of initiating him into, what to *me* is perfect happiness.

" Do me the favour to remember me most sincerely to Miss Grayson, who has set me raving with those two last beautiful songs, which I cannot get out of my ears ; and present my kind regards to Mr. Nobbatop, senior and junior.

    " Believe me, my dear Madam,

   " Yours, most sincerely and gratefully,

          " PEREGRINE BUNCE."

This was in due course despatched. Peregrine subsequently occupying himself in re-establishing himself in his lodgings, or, as he called it, in his letter, his "residence," until it was time to proceed to fulfil his engagement with his uncle. When the heart and mind are fixed upon any particular object, the day seems to stand still, and hours, which ordinarily flit away too fastly, hang sadly on hand. Peregrine, who had no pursuits, and, as we already know, no acquaintance, stayed in his own den until the clock should strike five —the weather not being particularly favourable for excursion.

That wished-for hour at length came, and at last out sallied Peregrine Bunce, and having reached

the Piazza in Covent Garden, mounted his way
to the Coffee-room, where he found his uncle
punctual to the minute, waiting to receive him.

" Hey gad," said the old gentleman, " well,
here you are—glad to see you—capital news
—one down t'other come on—eh ?—Pitched
battle by two men, as the old joke goes.—No
sooner beaten off from one place than on in
another. However, Perry, as we may have a
word or two to say to each other, come to my
room—all snug and quiet—good fire—double
doors—fog shut out—fine view of the market—
come along."

Saying which, the old gentleman led the way
to his apartment — an exceedingly good and
comfortable one—in which they found Limpus
very cosily installed in his master's arm-chair,
but who most properly and dutifully resigned
the post of warmth, upon the approach of his
said master and nephew, and then forthwith
bowed himself out of the chamber.

" Sit down, Perry—sit down," said Uncle

K 6

Noll—" there, there, draw in—snug and comfortable—no bad quarters for me, eh?—I like them—there—well now—and so—you've made another hit?"

" Yes," said Peregrine, " such a hit—and if you'll pardon a pun—such a Miss—nothing in the world can be more charming."

" And the fortune, eh?" said Noll.

" The best that has ever yet presented itself to *me*,"said Peregrine—" forty thousand pounds at the least."

" Pretty, you dog, eh?" said Uncle Noll, poking out his right foot, with the view of hitting Peregrine's shins.

" Pretty as I have described her," said Peregrine,—" and such a temper—so good natured —so unaffected; and, as I have told you in my letters, so far and away superior to the widow."

" —— I say," interrupted Uncle Noll, "have you quite cleared off Kitty, eh?—Oh you sly dog—you never told me of *that*."

" It was a youthful indiscretion, Sir," said Peregrine ; " but I would not worry you about it. Thank heaven, without annoying you, I have settled the whole of that business, and placed the poor dear girl in a position of comfort—I may say, happiness."

" You are a good fellow, Perry," said the uncle,—" and I tell you what, Perry,"—and here the old gentleman wiped a tear from his eye—" you sha'nt lose by *that*, my boy—good fellow—good fellow."

And as he repeated these words, he held out his hand to his nephew, and took his nephew's hand in his, and shook it—ay, and pressed it.

" Very excellent people, the Nobbatops," said Peregrine, (acting remarkably well, so as to infer his wish that his uncle should not load him with praise for doing an act of common justice,) " they are exceedingly anxious to have the pleasure of seeing you at Slambury Park— they really *are* the kindest, most hospitable, and friendly family upon earth."

" Hey gad, what !" said Oliver Bunce, " I
shall be very glad—but, I say, Perry—no more
stray governess — what I hate, those sudden
bursts, upsets—don't you see ?"

" I am now confident," said Peregrine, " nothing more of *that* kind can happen—still I
should advise you not to go down there just
yet.   It is a charming place, and nothing can
be nicer ; but I think it is *raather* damp in the
autumn."

" Hey—gad—damp," said Uncle Noll, as nephew Peregrine knew he would say,—" no, no—
then make my excuses.   I can't—no—changing
beds—and in the country—no, no ; you'll manage for me.   Of course, when business renders
it necessary, and all that, I'll go ;—but, I say,
when do you think things will come to a head
—as the old cockney joke goes, when will be the
bridle day, to lead her to the *halter*, eh ?"

" That, I think, depends upon circumstances,"
said Peregrine, " but it would, as I look at the
matter, be desirable, and I see no difficulty, if,

in arranging matters, George Nobbatop's marriage with Miss Screecher, and mine with Maria Grayson might take place simultaneously."

" You are sure you have bagged your bird ?" said Noll.

" Why," said Peregrine, " it has generally seemed to me, that so much in the way of acceptance is done, before one word of proposal is spoken, that I have always wondered at hearing that any man was ever refused by a woman. Surely nobody would make an offer until, by continued association with the object of his affections, and by an appreciation of her manner towards him, he was quite sure of being accepted ; as for myself —— "

" —— Why," interrupted Noll, " Miss Dory —— "

" Oh," said Peregrine, " that is quite a different matter. I cared for neither of those creatures, and I could hardly be surprised at the pert rejection of such a girl ; but I am speaking of things generally ; and I have no

doubt—nay, my dear uncle, I am perfectly
certain, that the amiable, pretty, lively, and
accomplished black-eyed Houri —— "

" What d'ye call her ?" cried Uncle Noll.

" Houri," said Peregrine, " is entirely my
own."

" Well, my boy," said Uncle Noll, " we shall
be all happy together ; that *is*, if her uncle con-
sents, and we can come up to his mark ; and
I shall see you, as I wish, ' *settled at last.*'
And now what shall we do with ourselves to-
day ?—where shall we dine ?—no dinners here,
as you know ;—you don't belong to any club—
that's bad ; however, we'll see about that—two
or three good houses close by—under our Piazza
—all dry and domestic—so, if you will just go
into the coffee-room, and wait while I make a
slight change in my dress, we can arrange our
future plans without much difficulty ; and I'll
stand treat, Perry, for as much claret as you
can drink in toasting your pretty black-eyed
Maria—what ?"

" Grayson," said Peregrine.

" Grayson," echoed Uncle Noll, " you won't find me flinch, my fine fellow, neither in that, nor in trying to make you comfortable with her. I have taken care to inquire about Nobbatop— great man in the city—splendid concern—he an excellent fellow—and you, a lucky dog. So, go—you can find your way, and I won't keep you a quarter of an hour."

So Peregrine went, and Noll rang for his trusty Limpus, and Peregrine betook himself to the coffee-room, as every room, whether in a club or hotel, is called, in which, as has been before observed, coffee is seldom or never drunk, and so, by way of whiling away the time, he asked one of the waiters for an evening news- paper. The paper was with obsequious civility supplied to the " fortunate youth," who caring, in the plenitude of his own happiness, very little for what the rest of the world was doing, skimmed over the fates of empires, the destinies of monarchies, and the disgraces of

ministers, which are predicted off hand by the
gentlemen of the press ; and carelessly cast his
eyes over the numerous rail-road accidents, and
lists of missing heads and limbs for which
rewards had been offered ; as well as over the
philanthropic appeals—personal applications to
the editor, to state that Mr. Wallis's name was
spelt " Walys,"—that the plaintiff's name, in
such a case, was Holloway, instead of Holway ;
and a variety of other equally interesting com-
munications, and listlessly threw down the jour-
nal, when, in its fall from his hand towards the
table, one word caught his eye, which suddenly
rivetted his attention.   The word was a name—
the name of a friend—he caught up the paper
again, and read—·

" CITY.—We are deeply concerned to state,
that in consequence of some sudden, severe, and
unexpected losses, the eminent house of Nobbatop, Snaggs, and Widdlebury, was compelled
to stop payment this morning.   The confusion
this unlooked-for event has caused, is inde-

scribable in the mercantile world. It is at the moment impossible to calculate the liabilities of the firm, nor the extent of ruin which its failure must involve; but we fear, from its very extensive engagements, that the results will be most disastrous. We ought to state, upon authority, that the report of Mr. Nobbatop's having absconded, is wholly unfounded."

" Well," said Uncle Noll, entering the coffee-room at this precise moment, and coming up to Peregrine in his most cheerful and lark-like mood, " come, I'm ready—we'll go to Richardson's—get our dinner—best house in London for a rump-steak—and then, hey gad, if you like, go to the play —as the old joke says, ' all work and no play makes Jack a dull boy,'—what !"

" Play, Sir," said Peregrine, " there is no play for me, now but a tragedy."

" Hey gad," said Noll, " what's in the wind now?—another governess—more Kitty Catherals?—what !"

" Read *that*, Sir," said Peregrine, throwing the paper to his uncle.

" Read," said Noll, " I can't——I hav'nt got my barnacles——read it *to* me, eh ?——what is it ?"

" I cannot read it, Sir," said Peregrine,——" I should expose myself if I attempted to do so."

" Well but tell me, eh ?——tell me," said Uncle Noll.

" In a word, Sir," said Peregrine, " my excellent friend. Nobbatop is ruined.——House stopped payment——misery, wretchedness, and all that—— as for dining anywhere, it is out of the question. ——I must go home——I must——what next to do I scarcely know."

" Well, well," said Noll, " but that's all nonsense——if your friend has broke, you can't mend him again by not eating——gad, as the old joke goes, ' a man who has no stake in the country, can't do without a chop when he is in town.'—— So, he's squashed, eh ?——that's it."

" Yes," said Peregrine, " I am not surprised

—the wasteful style of his living—his expensive table—his fine wines, which his position in life certainly did not justify — his pictures — his horses—his carriages ; the whole establishment. Failures like these are little better than frauds ; besides, the man himself was not two removes from a fool, taken out of his own sphere, in which, as it seems, he was little better. I always thought things were going wrong ; certainly, as far as civility went, they were all remarkably kind in that way. However, my dear uncle, I must beg off, as to dinner ; for I must get home to my lodgings, where I left a letter for the post, which, if I could, I would rather stop."

" Too late, Perry," said Noll, " since the convenient alterations in the post-office, for the benefit of the public, you have two hours less time to write in—your's must be gone."

" At all events," said Peregrine, who was dead beat by this *éclaircissement*, " I really cannot dine anywhere ; forgive me—but it requires a little serious consideration, as to what is the

best step to take ; and I must—I must intreat
you to excuse me till to-morrow."

One of the most painful parts of Peregrine's
mishaps appears to be the fact, that whenever
he fancied himself at the apex of success, he
always, as we have just observed, exerted himself to bring the triumphant issue of his proceedings under the immediate notice of Uncle
Noll. Here again was a defeat—decided, on the
face of it ; but, he still must have felt that he
had won the heart of Maria Grayson ; for of
that fact, there could be no question.

" Now," said Uncle Noll, " I can make all
allowances for the strength of your feelings,
Perry ; and I don't want you to do a violence to
them, by dining with me in a public coffee-
room ; but tell me—tell me now—how do *you*
really feel about the black-eyed girl, Maria ?—
what d'ye call her ?"

" Grayson," said Peregrine, " Grayson is her
name."

" Well but, you say she likes you," said Noll.

" I think she does," replied Peregrine.

" And you like *her* ?" asked the uncle.

" Why that is just *it*," said Peregrine,—" I *do* like her, and if this infernal affair had not happened, I might, in time, have loved her ; but, accustomed as she has been to a certain line of life, and a style—not perhaps of society—but of establishment, she would only be made miserable now, by being brought into the sphere in which, as my wife, she could only move."

" Ah," said Noll, " then you would sacrifice your own affection for her comfort ;—there, Perry, you show yourself what I have always thought you, a disinterested, kind-hearted fellow —to be sure—to be sure—she *has* lived splendidly."

" Absurdly so," said Peregrine, " I wrote to you about their mode of carrying on the war— and the stables—and the shooting—and the boating—and the carriages ;—it is all quite disgusting ; and if other people are to be ruined by such failures, I go the length, Sir, of calling them felonious."

" You are right," said Noll, " that's the high principle ; you may have your errors, Perry ; but you take the true view of matters ; and so do as you like this evening, and let me see you in the morning, and then we will talk more of this affair ; more will come out, and you will then see your way better ; so, good bye— don't worry yourself—things are not always so bad as they look at first ; as the joke goes, ' old Nick sometimes is not so black as he is painted.' "

So parted the uncle and nephew ; the uncle to his dinner—the nephew to his lodgings. The letter was gone—but Tim was at home ; and to Tim was entrusted a special mission to be executed forthwith, by means of the South-ampton rail-road that evening, or early the next morning, which had for its object the bringing away from Slambury Park, Mr. Peregrine

Bunce's clothes, dressing-case, and other effects, which he was to get from the superintending servant of the house, without the knowledge, of course, of Mrs. Nobbatop, or anybody else, and by which extrication of his worldly goods, he might, on the following day, be completely clear of the wreck of which he had so feelingly descanted to his jovial relation.

What the newspaper announced with regard to the failure of the house of Nobbatop, Snaggs, and Widdlebury, was, strange to say, true. It was a failure most tremendous, and complete —a continued perseverance in speculation upon speculation, holding *this*, for a rise in price, to effect which, came the necessity of selling *that* at a loss,—enormous dealings in funds, beautiful to look at, but fatal to touch—enterprises of a character and to an extent scarcely conceivable by ordinary minds, had at last brought them to an end from which there certainly appeared no redemption.

Mrs. Nobbatop—and how women, good ex-

cellent women, bear these tremendous reverses—
received the news of their fall as she would any
ordinary intelligence of the day.   Her husband
was, although unfortunate, honoured and honest.
Not a shadow of blame was cast upon him, and
her first movement upon the occasion was to
inquire whither they were to remove from Slambury — what furniture might remain at their
disposal, to be useful in a smaller residence; and
her first remark was, that all reasonable people
preferred small rooms to large ones, even in
large houses,—that wealth was the parent of
innumerable responsibilities, and that servants
were plagues and torments.

"My dear husband," said she, "I certainly
love this place, and beautiful as it is, it is dearer
to *me*, because it has been chiefly made by you ;
but when we began life, we had no such home
or establishment.   Why should we care about it
now ?—Thank God, my good kind dear, you
are well in health ; no man accuses you of
wrong ; you have an affectionate wife, who will

do all she can to cheer and comfort you ; and
Providence will be just if we deserve its goodness. Come——here is our Maria, ready to aid
me in any and every work that is necessary to
be done."

" Ah !" said the agitated master of the house,
taking Maria's hand, and pressing it to his lips,
" our dear Maria !"

Never perhaps was such a scene of rivalry in
domestic affection exhibited, as when the real
truth was developed ; nor ever a display of sin-
cerer regret and respect made, than by the
numerous servants of the establishment, when
the break-up was announced to them. Of course
an establishment like that of Slambury naturally
rolls on its usual course for a week or so, without any visible change, whatever may be the
alteration in the circumstances of its head, and
therefore there was no immediate ejection or
overthrow, although, when the fact of the bankruptcy had been proclaimed in the public papers,
further concealment was impossible.

The high eulogiums upon the mercantile and private characters of all the partners in the firm, and the unqualified testimonies to their honourable dealings, of course, alleviated the fall ; but Mrs. Nobbatop, cheered and delighted by such evidence in favour of her beloved husband, could not help murmuring to Maria, that she believed the whole of their misfortunes to have been the result of the influence of Mr. Saxby Mumps, a man she never could endure, and whose power over Mr. Nobbatop she had always dreaded.

It may sound strange, but it is not more strange than true, that there is an intuitive intelligence in women, which directs their attention to points of character and attributes in the minds of men which do not strike their male associates. Nobbatop looked upon Saxby Mumps as his tutelar deity ; and *that*, with all his mercantile experience and extensive knowledge. From the moment Mrs. Nobbatop first saw him, she pronounced her opinion of him to Maria. She set him down for a double-faced, under-handed speculator, and was never so well pleased as when he did *not* honour Slambury with a visit.

The failure of our poor dear friend Nobbatop and his partners was a plain straight-forward failure ; nothing contrived or connived at, in the way in which, if we are to believe that most admirable painter of nature, Foote, such matters were managed some sixty or seventy years ago.

In Foote's comedy of the " *Bankrupt*," one of his plays which might be acted in the most fastidious times, occurs the following scene, dependent upon the embarrassments of one Sir Robert Riscounter. It is quite worthy of attention, not only as illustrative of the manners of the day, but of the talents of the writer.

In a room we find two worthies of the names of Pillage and Resource, *tête-à-tête* :—

" Take my word for it," says Mr. Resource, " in the whole round of the law, and, thank

Heaven, the dominions are pretty extensive—
there is not a nicer road to hit, than the region
of bankrupts."

" I should have thought it a turnpike," says
Resource, " for, you see how easily a country
attorney can find it."

" Pshaw !" cries Pillage, " what, amongst ma-
nufacturers and meagre mechanics?—fellows not
worth powder and shot : and yet these paltry
provincials, Master Resource, are often obliged
to solicit my aid."

" Indeed !" says Resource.

" Why, t'other day," says Pillage, " a poor
dog, over head and ears in debt, from the country, was recommended to me by a client.   The
fellow had scraped together all he could get,
with a view of running beyond sea, but I stopped
him directly."

" Really ! ——"

" Yes," says Pillage, " in a couple of months
washed him as white as a sheep just shorn—
made him take a house in Cheapside, called him

a citizen in the London Gazette, and his name of John Mudge being as common as carrots, not a soul in the country suspected it was he— passed a few necessary notes to get him number and value, white-washed him and sent him home to his wife."

" Cleanly and cleverly done," says Resource.

" When the country chaps," says Pillage, " brought in their bills, he pulled out his certificate, and gave them a receipt in full of all demands, and now he is in business, and doing uncommonly well, for I left him two hundred pounds out of the six he brought with him to begin the world with credit again ; but," continues he, " I see *you* have found a remedy for Master Monk of the Minories—how did you manage that ?"

" Got some friends," says Resource, " to advance him cash on a project to monopolize sprats and potatoes."

" And it took ?" asks Pillage.

" No fear of that," answers Resource, " the

people of this country are always ready to bite at a bubble ; but, as a body, we shall break before the season for sprats ; and as to the potatoes, of which we laid in a ship-load or two, they are all in our cellars in Southwark, and have shot out branches as tall as the trees in the park."

At this pleasing description of probable re- sults, the worthy Pillage laughs, and inquires of his friend, *àpropos des bottes*, what he thinks the object of Sir Robert Riscounter's invitation is ? —upon which point, Resource, being aware of what he calls " a pretty large crack," satisfies his friend ; and a minute or two after, Sir Robert himself appears, and states that he has sent for them, to ask their assistance ; that his affairs have come to a crisis, and that, without some speedy and substantial aid, his credit will be gone.

Upon which this conversation ensues :—

" You surprise me," says Pillage, " I never guessed at a danger. Pray, Sir Robert, what brought on the disease ?—was it an alley-fever, or gradual decay ?"

"A complication of causes," says Sir Robert. "I, however, could have weathered them all, had the house in Holland but stood: their failure must be followed by more. Have you heard of anything to-day ?"

"No doubt of their stopping," says Pillage; "their bills were offered at Garraway's under forty per cent. As your name, Sir Robert, is not blown upon yet, suppose you coin a couple of quires—don't you think the circulation might screen you ?"

"No," says Sir Robert, "that mint is exhausted, and private paper is reduced to its primitive value. My real case can be no longer concealed—I must stop, and should be glad of your advice how to manage this matter."

"Why, Sir Robert," says Pillage, "there are two methods in use—the choice will depend on how your affairs stand with the world."

"Bitter bad, Mr. Pillage," says Sir Robert.

" I guessed as much by your sending for *us*,"
answers Pillage; " they treat us, Master Resource, like a couple of quacks——never apply but
in desperate cases——Now, Sir Robert, if you
find you are pretty near on a par, with a small
balance per contra——summon your creditors, lay
your condition before them, convince them you
have a fund to answer all their demands, and
crave a respite for three or four years."

" This," says Sir Robert, " will only be de-
laying the evil."

" That," replies Pillage, " depends upon how
you manage the cards. Don't you see, the
length of time, with the want of money for
trade, will induce the bulk of your creditors to
sell their debts at a loss of thirty or forty per
cent."

" But," says Sir Robert, " how shall I profit
by that?"

" How!" cries Pillage, " what hinders you
from privately buying them up yourself!——a fine
fortune saved out of the fire; and talking of

fires, for a present supply, you may burn a warehouse or two after they have been gutted of their contents, and so recover the full amount of the insurance." *

To all these suggestions, and that of secreting all the portable stuff—such as jewels, and cash, Sir Robert gives a decided negative, and concludes his negotiation with his councillors by denouncing the system of fraudulent bankruptcies, which at that period appear not to have been uncommon, and declaring that, however much men may suffer from his calamities, they never shall suffer by his crimes ; a declaration which, as may easily be supposed, draws down upon him the most violent invectives from his advisers.

Butler's notions of bankrupts and bankruptcies in *his* days were not very widely different from those of the modern Aristophanes. Butler says—

" A bankrupt is made by breaking, as a bird

L 6

is hatched by breaking the shell. He gains
more by giving over a trade, than he ever did
by dealing in it. He drives a trade, as Oliver
Cromwell drove a coach, till it broke to pieces.
He is very tender and careful in preserving his
credit, and keeps it as regularly as a race-nag
is dieted, that in the end he may run away with
it ; for he observes a punctual curiosity in per-
forming his word, until he has proved his credit
as far as it can go ; and then he has catched
his fish, and throws away his net ; as a butcher;
when he has fed his beast as fat as it can grow,
cuts the throat of it.

"When he has brought his design to per-
fection, and disposed of all his materials, he
lays his train, like a powder-traitor, and gets
out of the way while he blows up all those that
trusted him. After the blow is given, there is
no manner of intelligence to be had of him for
some months, until the rage and fury is somewhat digested, and all hopes vanished of ever

recovering anything of body or goods, for revenge or restitution ; and then propositions of
treaty and accommodation appear like the sign
of the hand and pen out of the clouds, with conditions more unreasonable than thieves are wont
to demand for restitution of stolen goods. He
shoots like a fowler at a whole flock of geese
at once, and stalks with his horse to come as
near as possibly he can, without being perceived
by any one, or giving the least suspicion of
his designs, until it is too late to prevent it ;
and then he flies from them as they should have
done before from him. His way is so commonly used in the city, that he robs in a road
like a highwayman, and yet they never will
arrive at wit enough to avoid it ; for it is done
upon surprise, and as thieves are commonly
better mounted than those they rob, he very
easily makes his escape, and flies beyond pursuit, and then there is no possibility of over-
taking him."

Infinitely more like the conscientious baronet in the play, than the imaginary bankrupt of Butler, was our worthy friend Nobbatop, who, when the blow fell, received it firmly but meekly, and immediately proposed to his nearest relations all the necessary steps to be taken in their altered situation.

Mr. Peregrine Bunce's servant Tim arrived at Slambury Park quite safe by the morning train or rail-road, and returned with his master's "things" and dressing case, umbrella, &c. &c., all which were carefully delivered to him by Mr. Nobbatop's own man, but who nevertheless thought it his duty to apprize his mistress, to whom he and all the rest of the servants were devoted, of the whole proceeding.

Maria Grayson was in the room with her aunt when the man stated the case. Mrs. Nobbatop merely smiled and said, " Oh, very well —you did quite right." Maria struggled with the strong feelings of a warm heart and generous mind, till he had shut the door, when, by an effort, she stammered out as it were——" Gracious Heaven !——is that possible ?"——and, throwing herself on a sofa, turned her almost convulsed countenance on one of the pillows, and moistened it with her tears.

CHAPTER XVII.

ONE cannot wonder at this natural burst of passion. The announcement of the callous heart-lessness of Peregrine's practical proceeding, following so closely as it did the receipt of his exceedingly affectionate, friendly, and compli-mentary letter, was not to be borne by a girl of high spirit and strong feeling like Maria, who had taught herself to look up to the venal for-tune-hunter as an agreeable and accomplished person, who, without premeditation or design, " prepense and aforethought," had, as the result of their—to *her* most agreeable—association, learned to esteem and regard him, and whose longer acquaintance with him would, most pro-

bably, have induced a more serious affection on
his part, which her heart had already admitted
its readiness to reciprocate.

And that this bright vision should be dissi-
pated and dissolved in so short a space of time
—that the devotion with which he had addressed
and treated her should have thus suddenly been
forgotten, nay, that the kindness and courtesy
of ordinary society, by which Peregrine's letter,
that very day received, was characterized, should
have curdled in a few hours into a cold-blooded
anxiety about a few clothes, a dressing-case,
and an umbrella, seemed far beyond anything
she could have expected in the conduct of any
man, but, least of all, from the favoured and the
favourite Mr. Peregrine Bunce.

A woman has—can have—no notions of such
debasement ; she, with her generous disposition, her confiding nature, and her utter ignorance of worldliness, full of feeling and reliance,
would risk all, lose all, worldly advantages, to
prove her devotion to the being who had once

established a preference in her heart, founded
upon what she considered a just estimate of his
qualities. If this Mr. Peregrine Bunce had
remained—not faithful, for that is not the word
—but remained as he *was*, eight and forty hours
before, Maria Grayson, in spite of the sudden
blow that had fallen, would have been as happy
to be his " co-mate in exile," or to have lived
upon the means they might together have commanded, as if she had been a queen. Bless her
—sweet girl—her's was a heart worth winning,
and this calculating slave had nearly won it :
but happy, probably, was it, that this unexpected
blight had fallen upon the fortunes of Slambury.
Who knows but that when once in possession
of the ease and comforts after which he was
always hunting, he might have neglected qualities which he had not the taste or feeling to
appreciate, and have driven a being, such as
Maria was, full of intellectuality, into despair
and misery, by the indifference which, in such a
person as Peregrine, was not at all unlikely to

follow the attainment—not so much of his idol—
as of her money.

It is hard, very hard to drive from the mind
and heart—if the heart *have been* touched—
of such a girl as Maria, the thought, the me-
mory, the love (?) which has been registered
and established there. Maria's pride, amounting almost to anger, for the moment placed
Peregrine exactly in his right position—but *then*
could she not find some excuses for him? Might
he not have sent for these things of his, for
some reason altogether disconnected with the
great cause of their ruin?—The truth is, if she
were not what is called in love, she was as near
it as young lady ever was, and no stronger proof
could be adduced of Mrs. Nobbatop's combined
judgment and feeling, than the fact that she
never once alluded to the conduct of Peregrine
Bunce, the real character of which (she not
being in love with him) was evident to *her*, from
the moment the butler mentioned the history of
the removal of his " things."

And now that Peregrine *has* gotten his
" things," and is again installed in his " residence," what is to happen? It may perhaps
have occurred to the reader, that when Uncle
Noll first heard of what is conventionally called
the " smash " at Nobbatop's, his impulse was
to secure Maria Grayson for Peregrine—his
look, the expression of his countenance, even
more than what he said, conveyed the idea
—and Peregrine himself was aware that it did.
But that was a fancy on the part of the old
gentleman not to be cherished by his nephew.
Maria was pretty, and nice, and accomplished,
and, moreover, as he knew, attached to *him*,
but he also knew enough to know that all his
uncle had to bestow would not be sufficient, according to *his* notions of things, to " carry on
the war," without a corresponding " come down"
on the other side.

Peregrine, practised as he was, not only in
enterprise, but defeats, felt rather uncomfortable
as to his morning interview with Uncle Noll.

He could not endure his " gibes and jeers,"
and, strange to say—or perhaps not so strange
—whenever any one of these discomfitures took
place, the greatest relief he found was in hurrying away from the scene of his disaster, and
flying across the country in some near direction.
However, the interview with Uncle Noll was
what a modern lexicographer would call " *un-
getoutofable ;*" so he therefore made up his mind
to the worst, and walked himself off to the
Tavistock Hotel.

" Well," said Noll, as his hopeful nephew
entered the room, " how are you, Master Perry?
—' well as can be expected,' as the old joke
goes ?—All true—dreadful crash—terrible tum-
ble—eh ?"

" Yes," said Peregrine, " it is a very sad
thing."

" Did you stop your letter ?" said Noll.

" No," answered Peregrine, " but I sent off
my servant early this morning."

" Right—right," said Noll, " to be sure, commiseration and condolence may do no real good ; but such attentions are felt. I anticipated what you would do ; people who have treated you so well deserve, at least, all the little kindnesses which you can pay them. They'll feel it, Perry—rely upon it, they will appreciate your conduct."

Nothing is more grating to the ear, or more discordant on the tongue, than unmerited praise or an undeserved compliment ; and what added to Peregrine's uneasiness upon the present occasion, was the recollection, through Noll's observation, that he might just as well have been civil, and apparently solicitous about the family at no expense, and just as safely and surely recovered his dressing case, umbrella, &c. &c. &c..

" However, Perry," continued the old gentleman, " this is no fault of your's ; you did not induce your friend Toppanob, or whatever you call him, to monopolize, and being in no degree accessary to the ruin of the family, I can't see why you should link yourself to its fortunes, or rather misfortunes. The girl, as a matter of course, was over head and ears in love with you."

" Not exactly *that*," said Peregrine, " I think she might have been won, and the thing perhaps settled ; but there is a certain flightiness about her manner, and a freedom in her conversation, which consoles me ———."

" What !" cried Noll, " for the loss of your friend's fortune ?"

" No," said Peregrine, " not for *that*, but for the breaking off of the connexion. It certainly is flattering to be well received ; and certainly forty thousand pounds are something in the scale ; but still, my dear uncle, with *my* feelings of devotion to simplicity and diffidence, I'll be hanged if I think I could endure what may be called a ' show-wife.' "

" Ah, Perry," said Noll, " our tastes are deucedly alike—I'm all for quiet—demure—eh gad, you—don't you know what I mean, Perry ?

—timid, gentle, retiring, and all that sort of thing."

" I quite enter into your feelings," said Peregrine, " and therefore it is, that I less regret— I mean as far as I am myself concerned," (when did he care for anybody else?) " that circumstances have so turned up as to hinder the conclusion of an affair which I begin to think might have led to future unhappiness."

" I've a notion, Perry," said Noll, " that you have a little touch of jealousy in your composition, eh?"

" No," said Peregrine, " not exactly jealousy; but I don't think I should like to see my wife looking too much pleased while talking to another man. What they do with their eyes is what would, as a husband, worry me. It is not so much the matter of their conversation as the manner; and now, even with Maria Grayson, whom I suppose, in all probability, I shall never fall in with again—I have sat upon thorns when I have seen her look kindly at a fellow called Towsey, a neighbour of their's, for whom she don't care one single sixpence, and at whom she laughed whenever he was absent—I can't bear that sort of ———"

" Ay, ay," interrupted Noll, " that's it—that's the ' green-eyed monster.' "

" Who," said Peregrine, " Towsey ?"

" No, no," said Noll, " Shakspeare's green-eyed monster, as the old joke goes ; rely upon it, you must be careful, cautious, wary, and wise, in *your* choice of a partner for life."

" I feel," said Peregrine, " that marriage must be, when there exists a congeniality of feeling, a sympathy in tastes, a sort of ———"

" I know," interrupted Noll, " I understan —you are right—rely upon it you are right— and it was because I never could hit upon any-thing suitable to myself, that I never married. —' Bachelors' wives,' as the old joke goes, eh gad !"

And during this dialogue, the old gentleman believed in the sincerity of his hopeful nephew,

and ended by rejoicing that——however adverse
in themselves——circumstances should have occurred to break off a match in which that
amiable young gentleman now declared himself
doubtful of securing the happiness he so dis-
interestedly sought to obtain.

As Spenser says——

> " What man so wise, what earthly wit so ware
>   As to descry the crafty cunning train,
>   By which Deceit doth mask in vizor fair,
>   And cast her colours dyed deep in grain
>   To seem like truth, whose shape she can well feign,
>   And fitting gestures to her purpose frame,
>   The guileless man with guile to entertain ?"

Never did there exist upon earth a better
practical illustration of Spenser's text, or a more
apposite reply to his pertinent question, than in
the case of the two men now before us.

Well——but now came the next point to be
settled——what was now to be done ? Now Peregrine regretted that he had re-betaken himself
to his lodgings——what was to happen?——here was
winter approaching, and that dull time of the

year in which London is perhaps the dullest of all miserable places of refuge. The natural answer to that inquiry would have been the cordial invitation of Uncle Noll to his comfortable ome, the use of his horses, carriages, dogs, guns, or whatever else he possessed, and the rational enjoyments of that oddly shaped little parlour, in which the reader was first introdueed to them ; but no—that was now taboo'd ground to Peregrine. There were the Mintons in force —the magistrate himself—his wife—and if not Mrs. Grout, at least Captain M'Larrup—" the boy with the bugle horn."

There is something like—at least poetical— justice, to place the feeling on no higher principle, in finding that the meanness and selfishness of our hero had not only lost him the object of his affections—as he called his anxiety for pelf—but, had even had the effect of excluding him from the hospitable residence of his too partial relation. As for Uncle Noll, he would not have cared for his coming down, and brav-

M 2

ing the storm ; but Peregrine could not bring himself up to the conflict, and so, for the first time for many years, he saw Christmas approach without having any very defined notion as to " whereabouts" he might enjoy its festivities ; a consideration not rendered the more agreeable by an anxious feeling which had taken possession of his mind, that his best chance of securing his uncle's post-mortem bounty, in case of his not being " settled" previous to his death, consisted in a perpetual attendance upon, and attention to him, carried to the full extent of shutting out the civilities of everybody else, he being fully aware of the devotion and assiduity with which worldly men sacrifice every other pursuit to that of pressing their visits and civilities upon their rich and single acquaintances, as they advance in age.

" I can't stand Twigglesford, Sir," said Peregrine.

" What not come to me at Christmas, Perry?" cried Oliver—" why if you never come again, come then—' Christmas comes but once a year,' as the old joke goes ; you must come too."

" The renewal of my intercourse with the Mintons would be the death of me," said Peregrine.

" But we don't visit," said Noll; " it was only on your account that I cared about making their acquaintance anything more than it had been for some time—pshaw !—come !"

" If you will forgive me," said Peregrine, " I would rather endeavour to get rid of the associations of the last few weeks, and go somewhere farther a-field."

" Forgive !" said Noll, " hey gad—what d'ye mean by forgive ?—do as you like—I have no doubt you find me a dull, and prosy, and ——"

" Ah, there it is," interrupted Peregrine, " that is exactly what I thought you would *say* —you *know*, my dear Sir, it is not so—one has feelings, and ——"

" There, there," said Noll, " I quite enter

into your views. It would be unpleasant for you
to be subjected to the remarks—and all that—
so—don't worry yourself, and I tell you how I'll
remedy the whole affair. I won't go home this
Christmas myself—there now ;—here we can
meet whenever we like. London's a large village, and ' nobody knows what his neighbour
does.' As the old joke goes, ' London is the best
place in the winter, and there is no better place
in the summer'—so here I stay—but, d'ye see,
I don't confine *you ;* but relieve your mind as
to my not being down at Twigglesford. I have
plenty of folks in town that I know, and being i
better health than usual, I'll stay—keep up my
hospitalities in the country as usual—' dispense
my presents without being present myself,' as
the joke goes ; and, in short, make a winter in
London, giving you full leave to wing your flight
in whatever direction you please, always hoping
upon the old principle of ' bad luck now, better
another time,' you may still find something suit-

able, for, by Jove, in the last three trials, it does seem as if there had been something like a fate about it."

" You are too kind to me, my dear uncle," said Peregrine ; " but now," added he—a bright thought suddenly glancing through his brain, " if you really do mean to stay in town, why not take my lodgings—there they are, perfectly at your service. The people of the house know me—know you, and respect you ; surely, it would be more comfortable than a hotel, and ———"

" You are a good fellow," said Noll, " an excellent fellow ; and I thank you for the offer : but I like this best ; here I am wholly independent ; my room and my servant are always ready ;—a capital breakfast—no necessity for dining at home, if you choose to dine out. No questions as to when you come in at night—or how long you are gone away—all free and easy, and bating the smell of the market, which at this time of the year comes to nothing, I like it amazingly."

Now, here the by-play between the two worthies is deserving of notice by those who care about looking a little closer than ordinary into human nature. Peregrine's exceedingly liberal offer to his uncle of his excellent lodgings, (or residence, as it was called at Slambury Park,) had its origin in his desire, under the change which had taken place in his circumstances, to get them off his hands. Uncle Noll's evasion of the generous proposition involved a point of considerable importance to Peregrine, inasmuch as the old gentleman laid considerable stress upon the independence of the hotel-life, in the course of which " no questions were asked as to when you came home at night—as to how long you were likely to stay away—where you were going," &c. &c. &c.

Peregrine had, as we know, obtained a sort of vague intimation from Limpus, as to the erratic, hebdomadal habits of his uncle, when he was in London, and had never since been quite at his ease, as to the influence which he fancied

might be in secret operation over his mind—
his doubts and apprehensions upon the point
were not at all weakened by the readiness with
which Noll gave up his prescribed, and regularly
acted upon, rule of rusticating at Christmas,
nor by the reasons which he offered for declining
the lodgings ; in which, if he had accepted the
offer, (paying for the same, be it observed,)
Tim would have been left with instructions
to ascertain at all hazards the destination of
Mr. Oliver Bunce, whenever he thought proper
to ruralize.

This scene was not unworthy of notice, but
neither Peregrine nor the reader, is likely to
get one inch nearer the real objects of these
periodical visits to some " undiscovered bower"
by anything that the elder gentleman of the
two is likely to let out. What preyed upon
Peregrine's imagination, was the apprehension,
knowing as he did, that something unpleasant
had happened in early life to some member of the
family, that the object of his uncle's punctual

and confidential attentions, (being, as indeed
Limpus had hinted, a relation of that said uncle,)
might be, as to consanguinity, nearer to the
old gentleman's fortune than himself ; or, at all
events, likely (because, in a family, the criminality of any of its members is universally considered as a misfortune,) to be favoured, much
to his disadvantage, by Noll, in the making his
will, provided that he could not bring about his
" settlement" before the old gentleman died.

So, here again was a new—indeed a double
excitement—a positive and negative impulse to
fresh exertions.   But which way was he to go ?
—where again was he to throw the handkerchief, where so few seemed willing to pick up ?
In the heartlessness of the man himself was to
be found the perfect readiness for a new start if
the line of proceeding could be pointed out ;
and as for that heartlessness, can a stronger
proof be required of it, that never once did the
thought of all his past happiness at Slambury
cross his mind, except when he felt inclined to

anathematize his unlucky stars for leading him into such a disappointment.

And what was doing at Slambury? As we have before said, such an establishment, by its own force and weight, must go on for some days without change or alteration. But the blow had fallen; and, as we have already seen, been met nobly by the mistress of the house. She—noble splendid woman—did not even adopt that which is supposed to be the wisest course in misfortune, bow her head to the coming wave; no, she held up against it, and let it dash past her unmoved and unhurt.

The scene at home, when Nobbatop imparted the whole history of the failure, occasioned by the resolute and determined monopoly maintained and persisted in, under the advice of Mr. Saxby Mumps, was, as may be imagined, dreadfully painful, more especially to him whose devotion to his wife and children—for child he called his adopted Maria—was earnest and exemplary. He endeavoured to qualify the abso-

M 6

lute necessity for their relinquishment of their
beautiful house, by saying that such a measure
was not immediately necessary; that they would
have time to look out for some other residence;
and that, although the arrangement of the
voluminous accounts of the firm would inevitably occupy a considerable period of time, still
he hoped eventually something might be saved
for them from the wreck.

His tenderness towards Maria, whose conduct
had been beyond all praise during the first dark
days of distress, was more than even that of a
father, had he really stood in that relation to
her.   The nobleness of her heart, and the splendid generosity of her character, had displayed
themselves in a manner even yet beyond the
reader's imagination.   She *was* a treasure.

" Have you heard," said Nobbatop, seeming
more alive to domestic matters than he ever
had been in the days of his prosperity, " from
our friend   Mr.   Bunce ? — I   am   exceedingly
sorry ———"

"Never be sorry about him," said Mrs. Nobbatop, "he has shown *him*self.";

"But," said the worthy husband, "surely you told me that Maria ———"

"Dearest, dearest uncle," interrupted Miss Grayson, "never mention his name again. The experience of the last three days has shown me how easily confidence may be misplaced, and how completely appearances may deceive."

"But what ———?" asked Nobbatop.

"Ask nothing," said Maria; "as he banished himself from this house at the earliest opportunity, so is he banished eternally from my mind. Had he ever possessed himself of my heart, I would have died rather than he should now retain it."

"But *his* heart," said Nobbatop; "I am no judge of these things."

"Heart, uncle," said Maria, "he has none; it is useless to worry you with the details of his conduct ; all I hope is, that never, never again shall I hear his name."

Poor Mr. Nobbatop, who came home tired and worried, and whose head was distracted with the complication of his difficulties, readily acceded to Maria's request, to hear no more of his worthy young friend ; and after a slight half dinner, half supper, retired to rest—or at least to bed—being obliged early in the morning to be again in the city.

And was it not painful and pitiful to hear him and his amiable excellent wife discussing, as they looked round their splendid rooms, which a few days since had blazed with lights, and rung with sounds of music, joy, and pleasure, how affairs had better be arranged, as to the disposal of the furniture, and whether it would not be more advantageous to have the sale of the pictures, and objects of *virtù*, in London. And is not the elasticity of the human mind one of the greatest wonders of our composition ?—One little week before, the idea of being turned out of this darling spot—the place of their own creation—the happy retreat from worldly care—the home of peace and comfort—would have gone well-nigh to break their hearts. The shock of ruin had destroyed them with an earthquake suddenness, and yet their minds survived the infliction, and, wounded as they were, contracted, —or perhaps one had better say, expanded— themselves into a calm and rational calculation of what was best to be done under " existing circumstances."

In the morning Mr. Nobbatop again went to town ; but, his own carriage, which, with the others of his establishment, was still at Slambury, took him only to the neighbourhood of the railroad station.—It was a wet—a dreary—sleety, snowy day ; what then ? he cared not for himself. His wife—his niece, were both at the door to see him off—to conjure him to take care of himself ; for although to the world he had now become nothing, he was more than ever all the world to them.

It was indeed a dull and dreary morning, and the ruts made by the wheels of the carriages, which had brought the kind and smiling, grateful visitors to Slambury during the preceding week, were flooded by the rain, which pattered against the windows, and rattled upon the roof of the conservatory, as if in mockery of the sorrow which prevailed within. Still, the attentive gardener was training and pruning, and turning round their frames, the choice plants, so recently the favourites of Maria, and still—justice be done to them, and praise be to them for it—the servants were more attentive to their mistress and Miss Maria than ever, and more solicitous to meet their wishes and obey their orders, than they had shewn themselves before.

The sound of a carriage aroused the attention of the fair inmates. No carriage appeared; but, upon an enquiry, it turned out that two gentlemen—and the kind-hearted butler called them gentlemen, without any particularly strong em-

phasis, wished just to look over the " premises."
—Who they were, or what they were, Mrs.
Nobbatop never inquired. She concluded that
the visit was something connected with the
general overthrow, and directed that they might
be admitted to see all that they required to see
of the house and its appurtenances ; she and
Maria retiring to their sanctum, which even the
law could scarcely invade ; which was a sort of
boudoir, a charming little octagon room, with
which Mrs. Nobbatop's dressing room and that
of Maria communicated, and in which, when
there was no company in the house, they generally passed their mornings.

What parts in the play the two mysterious
gentlemen performed, we know not. They certainly came with an air of authority, and
certainly visited the best apartments of Slambury, and looked at the furniture sagaciously
and appraisingly ; and one of them made me-
moranda in a book which he lugged out of a
side pocket. However, whether their intentions

were good or evil, time alone can unravel ; for, having taken their superficial survey, they thanked the trusty butler, who never left them, and retired.

Their departure was duly announced. Maria felt relieved—she scarcely knew why ; but her heart seemed lighter when they were gone.

It was not long after their secession, that the sound of horses' feet again awakened her attention—somebody was approaching—and then the noise died away. Whoever the visitors were, they had gone round to the stable yard. In a moment the thought flashed into her mind, that it was Peregrine—she had been deceived—or rather she had *not* been deceived in him ; but those who doubted him were the deluded ones.

It will do her no harm, poor dear girl, to admit that the thought, the hope, the expectation, that *she* had formed a just estimate of his qualities, cheered, animated, and delighted her. Some mistake of servants, so common of occurrence, had caused the confusion—he never

meant to desert and abandon them—he merely
sent for his dressing-case because he wanted it,
and would have brought it back the next day;
and his note was so kind, so good;—no, no—
it was quite impossible. She had been mistaken
—she had been led into renouncing and denouncing him; but here he was, to vindicate
himself against any charge of heartlessness or
worldliness, and much did she rejoice in the
happy result.

Scarcely had she satisfied herself that Peregrine had proved himself equally true in sun-
shine or in storm, when the butler—still acting
prime-minister, entered the room, and muttered
mysteriously, almost in a whisper, something to
Mrs. Nobbatop.

"Dear me, dear me," said the lady,—"but—
you know we do not receive visitors. We are
not—don't you see?—why *did* you let him
in?"

"He said, Ma'am," said the butler, "that he
knew you would not let in company, and there-

fore he came round through the stable yard to the servants' door. He says he won't detain you five minutes, Ma'am."

" Who is it, aunt ?" said Maria.

" Mr. Towsey," was the answer.

" Oh," said Maria, walking to the window to hide the disappointment which she could not have concealed had her countenance been visible, that it was *not* Mr. Peregrine Bunce.

" Well," said Mrs. Nobbatop, " have they lighted any fire in the library ?"

" Oh yes, Ma'am," said the butler.

" Show Mr. Towsey into the library, then," said Mrs. Nobbatop, " what he can have to say to *me*, and alone, I cannot in the slightest degree comprehend."

" So as he does not want anything to say to *me*, aunt," answered Maria Grayson, " I am not much interested in the affair." And again, as soon as Mrs. Nobbatop had left the room, Maria fell into a reverie, the object of which was a discussion with herself as to the proba-

bility or rather possibility, that Peregrine coul
really be the heartless creature which the *prima
facie* appearance of things seemed to prov
him.

When Mrs. Nobbatop entered the library, she
found her visitor, looking not altogether as was
his wont. He advanced towards her as she ap-
proached him, and held out his hand, which she
took, and felt to be remarkably cold—nay more
than cold, tremulous.

" Well, Mr. Towsey," said the lady, with her
usual air of cheerfulness, " sad things have happened since we last parted. Probably you have
not heard of my poor dear husband's sudden
misfortunes."

" Indeed I have," said Mr. Towsey, in a tone
unusual in his voice, " and that is what brings
me here to-day."

" Indeed," said Mrs. Nobbatop, " we are the
more obliged to you for your visit ; the world
generally keeps aloof from a falling house."

" My object," said Towsey—faltering in his

speech, and nervously agitated in his manner
—" my object, my dear madam—I—really—
scarcely dare venture to explain myself, for fear
of offending you."

" Assure yourself," said his companion, who
saw how natural and unaffected his agitation
was, " assure yourself that there is no chance of
offending *me*."

" I am placed," said Mr. Towsey, " in an
awkward and delicate position—and I feel the
difficulty I have to encounter. You are—you
must be—aware that for some time I have regarded Miss Grayson with feelings of admiration
—affection."

" I certainly am not ignorant of your feelings towards my niece," said Mrs. Nobbatop,
" but ——."

" Permit me to stop you for one moment,"
interrupted Mr. Towsey,—" permit me to add,
that I am fully aware of the nature of Miss
Grayson's feelings towards *me*. I know that my
attentions would be ill received, the offer of

ny hand rejected. I have therefore abandoned ny hopes with my expectations of success ; and that very circumstance it is that embarrasses ne at this moment."

" I really do not see what ——— " said Mrs. Nobbatop.

" Why that it is," continued the visitor, " our friends—nay yourselves—who may be more or less aware of the feelings I entertained for your charming niece, may attribute to other motives than those which really actuate me at the moment, the offer I am about to make to you."

" I still am at a loss to understand you," said the lady.

" I ——," and here again his voice faltered, " I —my object in calling—my only fear is offending by taking so great a liberty—my object in calling was merely to say, that if—if, and I feel I am taking a liberty in supposing the case—if there should be a necessity for your removing from this house—mine is—for as long a period as may suit your convenience, entirely at your service ; it does not emulate this charming place in accommodation or attractions, but as you have honoured me by visiting it, you know its merits and ———"

" My dear Sir," said Mrs. Nobbatop.

" Let me conclude," said Towsey, " in order to prove to you that I have no personally interested feelings in this offer, and that Miss Grayson may be convinced that I have no unworthy motives, and, moreover, that none of our kind friends and acquaintances may have an opportunity of making their remarks, I propose to leave it entirely at your disposal,—that is to say, I intend quitting home for Brighton for two or three months, and I hope, during my absence, you will find everything agreeable and comfortable at Blackford."

" Sir," said Mrs. Nobbatop, " what have we ever done, to deserve such generous conduct on your part ?"

" You have permitted me the pleasure of

your acquaintance," said Towsey, " I have been
constantly in the habit of receiving your hospitable attentions,— I have passed some of the
happiest hours of my life under this roof. The
offer I make is nothing. I should have felt no
earthly difficulty in proposing it, had it not been
for the consciousness of a more than implied
feeling towards your niece, which, however, my
sense and just valuation of my own qualities,
joined to a conviction that her affections were
otherwise engaged, have enabled me, if not to
conquer altogether, at least to control. This
it was made me nervous at first, but appreciating your kindness, and having, I hope, made
you understand my real feelings, I am now able
to press you to come to Blachford whenever it is
most agreeable, and consider it your own until
I give you ' notice to quit.' "

Mrs. Nobbatop was completely overcome by
the plain simplicity and natural earnestness of
Towsey's words and manner. She struggled
with her feelings, which had been fearfully

worked upon during the last eight and forty hours. Clasping her hands, and lifting her eyes to heaven, she said, or rather sobbed, for tears hindered her utterance,—" Thank God, we have at least one friend left !"

Towsey walked to one of the windows to hide his emotion.

" Come," said Mrs. Nobbatop, " come with me to our poor Maria ;—let me tell her of your kindness—let me ———"

" Not for the world," said Towsey. " It is the struggle of my life to conquer the unfortunate affection I once suffered myself to encourage. My object, therefore, is *not* to see her, especially under our present circumstances. I fear she is as dear to me as ever ; but I know my fate. I know my duty. It is in pure and sincere friendship I have paid you this visit. We must leave love to happier men ; and so, my dear Madam, what I shall do is this :— send over my man to receive your orders. To-morrow I start for Brighton.—Do whatever you

please.   Whenever it is convenient or desirable
for you to go to Blachford, go;—consider me
present;—I hope my housekeeper will treat you
well, and that my excellent friend Nobbatop will
find, if not such very good wine in the cellar as
I have tasted here, my butler will set, at least,
the best I have before him."

"But," said Mrs. Nobbatop, taking him by
the hand, "I can accept no such offer;—indeed,
kindest of friends, I am unable to answer you.
I know nothing of my poor husband's engagements, or what may happen; or ———— "

"I do," said Towsey; "I know that if nothing else comes out of the fire, his honour will,
purified by the process; but I know that some
temporary inconveniences must inevitably occur.
Therefore, give my regards and respects to
him, and press him to do what I ask.   I have
no relations—no cares—no debts—no responsibilities;—what I suggest to you is therefore to
be considered, as I have just said, only a mark
of friendship, esteem, and gratitude."

" And you will not ask poor Maria how she is ?" said Mrs. Nobbatop.

" No," said the excellent man with the unromantic name, " I dare not ; it is incompatible with what I consider just and right ;——present my compliments to her, and ——" here again his voice faltered, and passing his hand almost convulsively across his lips, he repeated——" I will send my man over to you to-morrow, to take your commands."

" But indeed," said Mrs. Nobbatop, " till my husband has authorized me to accept your kindness ——"

" He *will* accept it," said Towsey, " as why should he not ?——and if he do not, threaten him with my anger, and tell him that he is no friend of mine."

After some more parleying, Mr. Towsey shook hands affectionately with the old lady and departed, leaving her quite overcome by his generosity. Not a moment did she lose, as may be supposed, in hurrying to Maria

Grayson, and imparting to her the whole of the affair.

The disinterested generosity of his conduct, the delicacy yet clearness with which he had distinguished his affection for *her* from his friendship for the family, had their effect upon the noble-hearted girl. And she began to recollect the various good traits in his character, which she had noticed during their acquaintance, qualified as they always had been by the thoughts of his exceedingly unpicturesque person and remarkably uneuphonic name, and to contrast them with the various agreeable sallies of Mr. Peregrine Bunce, which, though very fascinating, and doing great credit to his head, afforded little, if any, evidence of the goodness of his heart.

" Isn't it uncommonly kind ?" said Mrs. Nobbatop.

" Indeed it *is*, aunt," said Maria, " and if I could separate it from any feeling towards us not stronger than friendship, I ——"

" Well," interrupted the aunt, " but I have

N 3

told you all—he does not mean to remain in the house—gives it all up ———"

" It *is* generous," said Maria ; and a host of recollections flashing into her mind, of his constant devotion to her, and her equally constant scorn and neglect of him,—" it is noble,"—and the tears flowed down her cheeks.

Some adepts in the art of lady-killing say, that if a man can make a serious woman laugh, he has carried his point to a great extent. To *us* it seems that he who can make the volatile lively woman weep, has even yet a better chance. In thinking over poor Mr. Towsey's conduct, which, be it always remembered, she could not believe quite disconnected from her own influence, she forgot his ungraceful figure, his unintellectual countenance, his plebeian name —she saw him, thought of him only as the sincere and generous friend of the family, such a one as she had hoped Mr. Peregrine Bunce might have been.

The question for consideration was, how Mr.

Nobbatop might think, as to the proposition. He, poor dear man, had no more idea that Towsey was in love with his niece, than he had that his niece was in love with Peregrine Bunce. Nothing, during his great career, either moved or excited him which was not somehow connected with his various schemes and innumerable speculations, and therefore Towsey's offer would come to him unshaded, unalloyed, and untainted, by any suspicion of a sinister design upon the girl, from any, the slightest imputations of which he had in his morning visit completely acquitted and exonerated himself. So that his wife, satisfied in her own mind of Towsey's honour and propriety, did not consider it necessary to preface her account of his proceedings with any reference to his admitted and self-avowed predilection for her niece.

"It *is* very kind of him," said the bankrupt merchant, "and his attentions are most seasonable; for at the moment, so sudden has been the blow, that I really do not know how I

should have been able to place you so comfortably ———"

" But, Sir," said Maria, " you know I have a
mode of ———" `

" Be quiet, my dear child," said Nobbatop,
" never mind your mode of doing things; although you are arrived at what are called years
of discretion, you are, as far as the world is
concerned, a child ; so, be patient, and quiet.
The Screechers have shown themselves, not
quite as I expected. I believe—I don't know—
but from what I can gather, it seems pretty
certain, that the marriage between George and
Miss Screecher will not take place ; so he tells
me, judging from letters he received this morning. If it is so, it shows how much of affection
there was in the attachment."

The words rang through Maria's ears—it was
a parallel case to that of Peregrine.

" For my own part," continued Nobbatop,
" ruined as I am—probably without a chance
of redemption—I would sooner George should

sweep the crossings of the streets, than accept
the trumpery fortune which the girl can bring
him, under the circumstances. Our position is
one in which real feeling, and real friendship,
are tested; and I hope he will act upon the
principle which I have advocated."

Again the words thrilled through Maria's
ears. What was this exclamation of her uncle's
but praise?—indirect, to be sure, of his worthy
and considerate friend, Mr. Towsey. She could
not help admitting the justice of what Mr.
Nobbatop said, and murmured almost audibly,
" What a pity he is *such* a man, and with *such*
a name !"

And what a pity, the reader may exclaim,
that Maria should suffer such considerations to
qualify the esteem and regard which such disinterested conduct demanded.

Nobbatop, who, although anxious to conceal
the extent of his misfortunes from his fond
family, was fully aware of the value of his neighbour's prompt offer, which it is therefore needless

N 5

to say, he determined first gratefully to acknow-
ledge, and then, thankfully accept.   It seemed
a sort of neutral ground, upon which, for some
time at least, those who were nearest and dearest
to him would be out of the range of fire, and
where, without a sudden transition to some
exceedingly confined residence, they might be
removed from the scene of spoliation which poor
Slambury was legally destined to become in a
few more days.

   But Nobbatop even then—and when he dispatched his letter to Mr. Towsey, was not aware
—nor did his provident wife even comprehend,
the extent of their neighbour's offer.   It is true
he had hinted at his intentions, but she had
not understood his meaning.   Not only was the
house to be at their service during the unsettled
period of their migration, but the establishment
as it existed.   He had said as much ; but until
his answer to Nobbatop's letter arrived, it had
not been made clear to the family, that they
were to consider themselves his visiters in the

most liberal and extensive acceptation of the word, he absenting himself merely to leave them more at their ease.

When Maria heard this letter read, her lips trembled, and tears filled her eyes. This conduct was so splendidly disinterested. And yet she could not blind herself to the truth, that it was for *her* sake it had been adopted. She made an effort to speak collectedly, in vain— she struggled. Her aunt saw her emotions.

" What, are you ill, Maria ?" said she.

" No, no," said the agitated girl, " this man's generosity is above praise. Why should he leave his house to make way for us !—if we *are* to be his visiters, why should he not remain ? *I* cannot say this ; but surely you may. Such a heart and disposition should be treasured and worshipped. I am not blind, nor insensible. Aunt, I know why he proposes abandoning his home while we are to occupy it. He thinks—he feels, that I shall consider the invitation as given for *my* sake, and for the sake of securing my society,

with which—I do not speak vainly—he has told
me, he is pleased and gratified. I will answer for
his being superior to any such view or motive.
He has proved himself so. Why should he leave
his home ? If we *are* to be his visiters, why
should we be left without our host ;——entreat
him to stay."

" You are an extraordinary girl, Maria," said
her uncle, " but your feelings here are right,
just, and proper."

" I only emulate *his*," said Maria ; " write
then, and beg him to remain and receive us."

" Maria," said Nobbatop, looking at her as if
astonished at the energy of her manner, " will
you write in our name ?"

Maria, after the pause of a minute, during
which she appeared to be struggling with her
feelings, said, in a firm and decided tone,
striking the table emphatically with her hand,
" Yes, Uncle, if you wish it, I WILL."

" But will it be right, Mr. N. ?" said Mrs.
Nobbatop.

" Leave her alone, my dear woman," replied her husband, " the heart that can suggest such conduct will never go wrong."

" No, aunt," said Maria, " I should not have adopted this course without consideration. I have been taught a lesson within the last few days, from which I may benefit much, and which will never be eradicated from my mind. My motives are good, therefore my conduct cannot be ill. Dictate, my dear uncle, and I will write."

" No, Maria," said her uncle, " write by my direction, but supply the words yourself. Women are greater adepts in the art of correspondence than men, except indeed in that style of correspondence to which my mind and labour have been for so many years, as it now turns out, most unprofitably devoted."

" I will do whatever you wish," said Maria. " Upon the question of his leaving his house at a season when his hospitalities are remarkable, I know I may speak ; and, putting aside all other feelings, I am sure, besides being more agreeable and convenient to *him*, it would be more satisfactory, and I may say respectable, that we should be really his guests, in his presence, than his tenants in his absence."

" Write what you please," said Nobbatop, " and say I authorize and desire it."

Away went Maria to perform the task, to the fulfilment of which, in its highest degree, she was resolved.

" That girl," said her uncle to his wife, as she quitted the room, " that girl has a mind fit for an empress. God bless her, poor child, how different are her prospects now, from what they were seven days ago ! Settled not only comfortably, but, as I may say, in comparative affluence for a woman. All is lost !—and her fortune shares the fate of ours. At present I see no ray of light ;—however, let us hope for the best."

" *I* always do," said the amiable lady of the house.

And what was Maria doing?—writing the following letter to Mr. ———. Why *had* he such a name?—Mr. Towsey:—

" *Slambury.*

" DEAR SIR,

" My uncle and aunt have desired me to say, that in their grateful acceptance of your kind offer of a temporary home at Blachford, they forgot to press upon you one point which is essential to their enjoyment of your friendly proposition.

" They consider that your quitting your house to make room for us, is a sacrifice which they cannot permit you to make. Nor would they feel half so comfortable, half so happy, or half so much at their ease, while you were away, as they should be if you were present, I will scarcely, under our circumstances, say doing the honours—but affording the kindnesses of Blachford.

" I am directed to beg you, if you will fill

the measure of your friendship and consideration, to remain at home—to receive us—since
you have been so good as to make the offer,—as
you would, in our better days have done ; and
so I write, secretarially; but if my own humble
request can have any effect upon you, I do not
hesitate to entreat you to remain at Blachford,
which would be to us a desert if deprived of
the presence of its master, whose nobleness of
generosity and disinterestedness of feeling, have
given us all the highest opinion of his heart
and character.

      " In the name of my uncle and aunt,
          " And in my own,
        " Believe me, Dear Sir,
      " Yours, faithfully and gratefully,
              " MARIA GRAYSON."

Maria showed this letter to her uncle, who
read it, re-folded it, kissed her cheek, and
desired her to put it in an envelope, and send it
directly.

Now, there are—for in the constitution of the world and society, there are minds capable of such dirty imaginings—there are people who would think—or, think is hardly the word—surmise, or suspect, that Maria Grayson, finding her fortunes fallen, was glad to reconcile herself to a match with the rich man whom she before had ridiculed. They who ventured so to guess, or insinuate, knew her not. No, with a high spirit and strong feelings, the heartless conduct of the man to whom she had conceded so much, forcibly as it struck her at first, when it came to be so suddenly placed in juxta-position with the unexpected liberality of his inferior rival, worked the miracle, and wrought the change. Maria, with all her pride and dignity, would in the very next week after the fall of her uncle's house, have applied all her accomplishments to the maintenance of their establishment, had it been necessary. Rely upon it, there are very few mercenary women in the world ; when they *are* mercenary, they are not the women to be spoken of, or written of. Woman, with all her power and influence over man, is the most patient, enduring, toiling, suffering being that ever was created. What words are there to be found in any language sufficiently strong or emphatic, to express our obligations and gratitude to them? Mark then—of such Maria Grayson was one.

Our poor bankrupt merchant was forced to return to London in the morning, not as heretofore welcomed into the city as the great director of all things to be done, and the great oracle of all that was to be suggested. He was to be examined, and questioned, and placed before a meeting of creditors, in company with his partners, of whom, let it be observed, Mr. Saxby Mumps was not one. He had been the adviser, councillor, and "friend," and to his exceedingly clever calculations and sapient suggestions, the downfall of the great firm of Nobbatop, Snaggs, and Widdlebury, was most unquestionably owing.

The result of eight hours' labour was not altogether satisfactory ; it appeared, after working like horses, and wading through all sorts of documents, that the affairs of the house stood thus :—

	£.	s.	d.
Liabilities .	964,382	13	4¾
Assets . . .	471,219	6	11½
Doubtful . .	118,714	3	8¼

Leaving upon the good and supposed recoverable debts, a deficit of 493,163*l.* 6*s.* 5¼*d.* which might be further reduced, supposing the doubtful debts were paid, to 375,449*l.* 2*s.* 9*d.* ; but *that* was the best to be made of it. The dividend, therefore, did *not* look promising ; although, as Saxby Mumps said when he heard of the wind-up,

" Good !—six in pound—do," and out he walked, pale, cold, and unmoved, as if he had had no share whatever in advising the enormous speculation, under which his dear friend and pupil had fallen into utter and irretrievable ruin.

It should be observed, in this calculation of
assets, the private estates of the partners had
been included, and Slambury, with its furniture,
" appurts, &c." had been set down at thirty
thousand pounds.   The chances were, it would
not fetch so much; but being doomed, poor Nobbatop, with tears in his eyes, naturally thought,
with redoubled gratitude, of the handsome and
liberal offer of his neighbour Mr. Towsey.

It may easily be imagined, that our poor
merchant, almost sneered at by his cold-blooded
adviser, came home that night, not in very
good spirits ; but it was beautiful to see, and
highly honourable to the class of persons to
whom the praise is due, how devotedly kind—
nay, we should say more than kind—devotedly
civil and attentive to him, were all his servants,
of whose conduct we have before spoken, who
were fully aware of the value of their tenure of
office in the house where they had been so long
and so liberally maintained and treated; but such
was his nature, such was his character, that the

very pressure of his misfortune seemed to raise the affections of the subordinates by whom he was surrounded.

The next morning brought, of course, an answer to Maria's letter. Read it :—

" Blachford,
" —— 18—.

" Dear Miss Grayson,

" Your letter, written by direction of your uncle and aunt, has given me much pleasure. I felt that by leaving this house at their disposal, I should best consult their convenience; but, assured as I am, not only on their parts, but your own, that they would not object to my receiving them, as I should at any other period of our acquaintance, I shall most gladly abandon my journey to Brighton, and endeavour to render my humble home as agreeable to my friends as possible.

" Still, dear Miss Grayson, make your uncle and aunt understand, that they are not in the

slightest degree to be interfered with, in their
arrangements, and that, although I shall have
the greatest pleasure in acting host, at all seasonable and reasonable times, you are all of you
to consider yourselves wholly independent of the
very humble person who happens to be master
of the house.

" With sincere regards to your uncle and
aunt, and very best compliments to yourself,

" Believe me, dear Miss Grayson,

" Your faithful servant,

" J. Towsey."

The tone and language of this kind and
sensible letter sufficiently proved—at least, so it
appears to us—that Mr. Towsey understood
Maria's letter, as it also appears most probable
she meant he should.   One thing is certain, that
she was not dissatisfied with it, but, on the contrary, all selfishness apart, felt gratified by his
determination of remaining at Blachford, because she was assured that the arrangement

would more conduce to the comfort of her uncle and aunt, and relieve them of a restraint which must be inseparable from the gratuitous occupation of a friend's house in his absence.

But Maria was destined to receive another agreeable letter on the same day, and one which really made her heart glad, not only for the news it contained, but because it exhibited human nature in a more favourable light than that in which her uncle had viewed it the preceding evening, and because it announced the certainty of an event upon which the happiness or misery of her favourite cousin George depended. As we *are* shewing letters, perhaps we may let that of Miss Harriet Screecher speak for itself :——

" *Splaydon,*
" ——— 184—.

" My dear Maria,

" It is impossible to describe to you the sufferings I have endured for the last three days, the dread and suspense in which I have lived, or rather existed, on account of our dear George. Knowing my father's extreme punctuality in matters of business, and the proverbial prudence of all his mercantile transactions, I saw nothing but the wreck of all my hopes in the melancholy event which has occurred ; and although he said nothing to me on the subject, and I dared not say anything to him, I felt assured that George and I were separated eternally.

" Poor dear George has written me two of the kindest letters that man could write ; but I could trace his desponding spirit in every line—his certainty equal with my own, that we were doomed to be parted for ever. Indeed, poor fellow, he mentions in one of his letters, or rather in a postscript, that he sees no chance for him but going to Australia, where some speculation—a word I have just now learned to hate—offers itself.

" Think then, my dear, dear Maria, of the joy which filled my heart this morning, when my

kind father called me into his own room, and told
me, that having so long sanctioned the addresses
of George, and having consented to our marriage, he felt that he should be acting cruelly,
and doing me and George the greatest injustice,
if he now revoked his decision. It is impossible
to describe to you what I felt at that moment.
The announcement was so unexpected—the decision so unhoped-for : how I expressed my
gratitude I cannot even recollect ; for all I know
is, when I recovered from the shock, I found
my dear tender mother bathing my temples,
while my father held my hands clasped in
his.

"When I was sufficiently recovered to listen
to details, my father explained to me the arrangement which he proposes, and which, I am
sure, you will think as kind, and generous, and
honourable, as I myself consider it. Our dear
George, from not having been in partnership
with his father, is not personally involved in the

insolvency of the firm ; he, therefore, is free ;
and instead of fulfilling the intentions which we
had formed when he should become a partner,
which he was to have been upon our marriage,
my father takes him as junior partner into his
own house, leaving the fortune which was
destined for me, in the business, and suggesting
our residing, for some time to come, here and
in town with him and Mamma.

" This is too much joy, dear Maria. The
habits of business for which our dear George
is so remarkable, and, as my father says, are so
exemplary, will enable him to relieve his future
Papa-in-law from a great share of the labour
which, after a long life of successful toil, begins
to tell upon his constitution, and I, dearest
Maria, am made the happiest girl in the
world.

" And won't you come to us, and stay with
us, whenever dear aunt and uncle can spare
you ?—won't they come too ? It is a bright

prospect that opens to my imagination; and I hope that you will not be worse off; for if ever there was devotion in a lover, your swain Mr. Peregrine Bunce—I wish he had a more agreeably sounding name—possesses it in a most eminent degree. I ask no questions, but I can give some answers. Papa says that his uncle is as rich as Crœsus, and so devoted to his nephew, that he only waits his bidding to do all that is noble and generous towards his niece elect.

" If I write nonsense—or what I should *not* write—pray, pray forgive me. I am too happy —just at the moment too when all my anticipations were defeated, all my fondest expectations blighted. I believe George will come down with my father to-day, at least he told me before he went, that he would ask him to do so.

" Write me a line, dearest sister—for so I almost consider you. Accept all our affectionate regards, and present them to aunt and uncle.

I leave you to detail my delightful news to dear Mr. Nobbatop, and entreat you to believe me, dearest Maria,

" Your's, affectionately,
" HARRIET SCREECHER.

" We heard this morning that you were all going on a visit to little Towsey's—is it so ?— Poor dear little man, how happy and proud he *will* be !"

Maria read this letter with infinite pleasure. It exhibited a noble generosity on the part of Mr. Screecher, and promised happiness to the fair writer, and to her cousin George. Of course she lost no moment in reading it to her aunt, omitting, however, two passages—one, that, in which allusion was made to the devotion of Mr. Peregrine Bunce—and the other, that in which Mr. Towsey was spoken of slightingly, and in a tone of ridicule. Nothing could—out of severe misfortune—have turned out better, than things seemed to have hitherto done. Before the end of the week, the Nobbatops were safely lodged at Blachford, and there were visited by the Screechers, while the attentions of the worthy host were exactly of the character which marks high breeding. Everybody under his roof was left perfectly independent, until the daily meeting at the dinner table, and during the domestication of the week which followed, a more intimate knowledge of his temper and character, and the assurance of his generosity of heart and kindness of disposition, had rendered him in Maria's eyes an object, to say the least of it, of esteem.

Sir Richard Steele tells us, that " handsome people are usually so fantastically pleased with themselves, that if they do not kill at first sight, (as the phrase is,) a second interview disarms them of all their power."—Taking the reverse of this, and moreover, bearing in mind the often quoted axiom of Sheridan, the reader may

o 3

fancy that the constant association of Maria
with Towsey—the daily evidence afforded of his
kindness and consideration towards his friends,
and his benevolence and charity towards his
poor neighbours, began to work a wonderful
alteration in her opinion of him.   To be sure,
his nose was not aquiline—his eyes were not
sparkling black—his dark locks did not cluster
over a high white forehead, and his little wisps
of whiskers were not particularly graceful.   His
figure was as unlike that of the Apollo, or the
Antinoüs, as may be imagined.   He was what
would be familiarly and colloquially called, a
" potty man ;"—but what should we care for
the material, or shape, or workmanship of the
casket that contains such an inestimable jewel
as an honest heart ?

While all these arrangements were in progress, and while the sun still seemed to shine
upon the ruins of the fortunes of the Nobbatops,
their friend Mr. Peregrine Bunce was still in
London—rather at fault as to his next exploit,

but still inestimably dear to his uncle, who thought him not only sharp and clever, but— which he valued more—good.

" I'll tell you what," said Noll, " you have behaved in this last business well—unwilling to drag a poor girl into uncertainty and difficulty ; besides, by your own account, I don't think she would have suited you, eh ?"

" I really think not, Sir," said Peregrine, " as I have before said, she is somewhat too lively in her manner, and, I should say, must be extra-vagant in her habits. You know *my* taste—the quiet, unpresuming—eh ?"

" Your uncle's fancy to a tittle," said Noll, " that's my fancy, as I said the other day, or rather was—for—ha! ha! ha!—it is rather gone by with *me*. My pleasure now is to see the en-joyment of others ; and I *do* hope, Perry—to be sure, you have been somehow unfortunate—but I *do* hope to see you settled before I go."

" Everything seems to show," said Peregrine, " that Nobbatop's conduct, as well as that of

his partners, has been highly honourable. I
hear the place, Slambury, is to be dismantled,
and all the furniture, and wines, and pictures,
and all that sort of thing, sold—a great portion
of the furniture on the spot—now, at this time
of the year, I should think things would not
fetch much, and there are two or three *objets*,
as the French say, which I think, my dear
uncle, would suit you. The billiard table is a
good one, and you want a billiard table; and
there are two cabinets, which Miss Grayson
used to call her's—poor girl—exceedingly handsome. I have no doubt they will go cheap;—
and he has got a pony, the best trotter I ever
crossed, which I always used to ride as a special
favour. I think we might nab that for next to
nothing."

" Gad," said Noll, " I see you have an eye
to everything."

" And," continued Peregrine, " their favourite
dinner service is just the thing for you. You
were going last year to buy one at Copeland's.

—You will get this for half the money.—Only
we must send some agent down, so that it may
seem that no gentleman is bidding."—(*Gentleman!*)—"I'll take care and get a catalogue, and
mark the lots—for I know them well enough to
know what you would like."

On the morning of the day succeeding this
characteristic dialogue with his uncle, Mr. Peregrine Bunce, in crossing Lincoln's Inn Fields,
happened suddenly to encounter Mr. George
Nobbatop. Their meeting was accidental, but
their greeting was cordial. George had been too
much engaged in business, to have thought of,
or if he had thought of, to have comprehended
the exact state of affairs between Peregrine and
his cousin Maria.

As inquiries are cheap commodities, and a
question of ordinary civility binds a man to
nothing serious, Mr. Peregrine Bunce asked
warmly and enthusiastically after Mr. and Mrs.
Nobbatop, and Miss Grayson ; in reply to which
he received for answer, the information, that

they had left Slambury, and had gone on a visit to Mr. Towsey's, at Blachford. Peregrine affectionately pressed the hand of Mr. George Nobbatop, and requested him to present his kindest compliments and regards to the family, all of which Mr. George Nobbatop promised to do.——And so *they* parted.

The break-up, or rather the break-down, of such an establishment as that of Messrs. Nobbatop, Snaggs, and Widdlebury, naturally caused, not only much confusion in the mercantile world, but much conversation in circles not immediately connected with the failure, and scarcely a day passed in which something did not come before the public, relating to what *was* to be, or what was *not* to be, done in the affair. However, as *we* know Peregrine had made up his mind——he had, to use a familiar, but very expressive phrase, " cut the connexion," and *that* too with his uncle's full consent, obtained, under the impression which he himself had made upon the old gentleman's mind——By so much the more mean and hypocritical was the warm reception which he gave George Nobbatop when he met him.

Peregrine Bunce was one of those half-and-half gentlemen who get their information, as to what is going on in society, from the newspapers. All the " we understands," and " we have heards," were imbibed by him as pure knowledge, and he pored over the list of " fashionable arrivals," including that of " Mr. Henry Bosh, at the Catanpan Hotel," or the departure of " Lady Slobberly from the Dodberry," with the deepest possible interest. However, in plodding over the Morning Post, which, besides all the chit-chat of the town, gives the parliamentary debates and law proceedings better than any paper going, about three days after his encounter with George Nobbatop, he found a report of a short case in the Court of Bankruptcy. Knowing nothing of law, and knowing nothing of the object of this particular matter, he merely read it because the peculiarity of the name of the party, caught his eye. The question raised, was one, as to the liability of our poor Maria Grayson's fortune, to the sweeping operatión of the insolvency of her uncle—it was decided in her favour—her fortune was out of the reach of all claimants ; and so honourably, in her favour, as regarded Nobbatop himself, that the creditors, if they *could*, would not have touched a shilling of it.

Peregrine read the decision — read Maria Grayson's name all printed and published at full length, together with the announcement of her possession of the capital sum of thirty-one thousand five hundred pounds (instead of the stated forty thousand) thereunto annexed, and of her legal and actual vested interest in it.

Then—and at that moment—did the love which had not been quite extinguished by the damp of Nobbatop's distress, begin to crackle, and almost blaze again.—" I have won her," said Peregrine—" she loves me.—I have retired because I had not the means to support her as she ought to be supported. She will appreciate those feelings ; and I will lose not a moment in flying to her—sweet innocent. What a blessing to such a creature must this decision be ; and how happy shall *I* be, if I am not too late, the first to announce this happy result."

Peregrine was again on the alert. Tim was ordered to have everything ready for a start ; and as his master knew from George that the family was domesticated at " Spooney Towsey's," he was perfectly aware of the road he had to take.

He did take the road, and arrived at Blachford in due time. Mrs. Nobbatop, for whom he first enquired, received him with all her usual courtesy, and acknowledged his kindness in coming to ask after them. She knew that Maria had received him favourably. She had also heard her censure, and even denounce him ; but she only looked at him as the agreeable visiter at Slambury, and thought he would be an acquisition to their little party ; and, moreover, as the quarrels of lovers are but the renewals of love, there was, as she fancied, every probability that Maria and he would be friends again.—— Whether with, or without the performance of a certain process, which proverbially forms part of the ceremony of such reconciliations, it is not for us to surmise.

Mrs. Nobbatop, dear soul, when she so kindly received the hypocritical sneaking Peregrine, was not aware of what had taken place that morning before his arrival at Blachford.

On that morning Mr. Towsey had heard the decision in favour of Maria and her fortune. Details of love scenes, since the world has gotten beyond the mawkishness of mock solemnity, are dull and tiresome ; and even if they be not, to the lovers of sentimentality, such a scene as occurred between Mr. Towsey and Miss Grayson would afford no kind of gratification.

After breakfast, the homely host and the fair

visitor, were left alone. In his manner, at the best of times shy and embarrassed, there was something at the moment which she remarked as peculiarly strange, and, accordingly, she made some common place observation, and was leaving the room.

" Miss Grayson," said the master of the house, " will you permit me to say a few words to you ?"

" Of course," said Maria, " why should I not ?"

" I feel," said he, " that I am violating a rule which I laid down for my conduct when you first honoured me with your company here. I admitted to your aunt, the strength of my feelings towards you, and I assured her that that strength of feeling should never exhibit itself during your stay, and, in order to avoid the possibility of annoying you, I suggested my leaving the house. Forgive me—pray forgive me—when I say that your kind letter—

to me the most valuable letter I ever received
—gave me hopes, that after a longer acquaintance, you might be induced to think better of
me than you had previously done."

" Indeed," said Maria, " you quite mistake
my feelings. Nobody do I more esteem and
regard than yourself; and each succeeding day
that I am here, affords new proofs of your kindness and liberality."

" Maria," said he, looking—as sincere love
will make even a plain man look—inspired,
" Maria, if I may so call you, our letters to-day
announce the blessed—for so it is to me—
decision, that your fortune is secured to you."

Maria fixed her dark penetrating eyes on his
countenance, with something like wonderment at
this allusion.

" You are therefore safe from the ruin of
your house," continued he, " and mistress of an
independent property."

Maria turned pale—her lips quivered—and

he asked herself, " Have I again been deceived?
—are all men mercenary alike ?"

" That," said her companion, " to me is every-
hing. Thank heaven ! *my* fortune is ample—
ny income far beyond my expenditure. Yes,
Maria Grayson, I am rich. On my knees I
mplore you to accept my heart, which has
so long been devoted to you, and afford me,
besides the blessing of calling you my own,
the happiness of appropriating the whole of
your income to the use of your excellent uncle
and aunt, so long as they live. I want none
of it ; and if——if I am so fortunate, with a
perfect sense of all my personal demerits, to
obtain your sanction to this hope of my heart,
I—I ——"

Maria Grayson, as the tears streamed from
her eyes, faltered out, " I was *not* deceived in
you." She could say no more ;—her head sank
upon his shoulder—he pressed her to his heart.
—He deserved the prize he had gained.

Of the particulars of this brief scene, and of

its necessary results, Mrs. Nobbatop was in
perfect ignorance, when our friend Peregrine
made his appearance. ·

" Charming place," said Peregrine to the old
lady, " not quite up to Slambury, but very
pretty.— Maria quite well?— I suppose little
Towsey is at home, eh ?"

" We will ring, and see where they are," said
Mrs. Nobbatop. " Mr. Towsey has got two or
three friends down here to-day ; so if he should
ask you to stop, you will find it livelier than
usual."

When the servant was dispatched to Maria,
to announce Mr. Peregrine Bunce's visit, her
first resolution was not to see him; but Mr.
Towsey, whose confidence had naturally grown
with success, entreated her to accompany
him to the drawing-room, to see this splendid specimen of humanity, whose appearance
there, Maria, as well as Towsey, instantly and
properly attributed to the decision as to the
young lady's fortune.

Mrs. Nobbatop, whose mind was, as we know, the purest and most unsophisticated imaginable, could not at all account for the exceedingly warm and rather facetious manner in which her niece and Towsey treated Peregrine. They affected to be so delighted to see him, wondered where he had been so long, and enquired after his uncle with a sort of preternatural affection. Peregrine was too quick not to perceive that he had decidedly " missed his tip," and that, although the aunt was still as seriously kind as ever, the niece and her companion were acting upon quite another plan. He began to get proportionably fidgetty, and made some sign of going.

" Oh," said Mrs. Nobbatop, " you won't go till you have had some luncheon. To be sure, I am taking a great liberty in your house, Mr. Towsey; but ———"

" Don't mention it, my dear Mrs. Nobbatop," said Towsey, " we shall be too happy. I am only waiting for the return of our friends from their walk.   These new married people are so loving."

" Talking of your uncle, Mr. Bunce?" said Maria, " when are we likely to see *him?*"

" Why," said Peregrine, quite aware that he was somehow found out, " I told you I thought it not very likely he would be prevailed upon to leave London just at this season of the year."

" Is there any news in town?" said Towsey, with an air, and in a tone, which a person so quick as Peregrine could not fail to understand and appreciate.

" Not that I have heard," said Peregrine, who knew too well the expression of Maria's bright eyes, to be at all comfortable, when he saw a certain exchange of looks between her and his host.

" I thought," said Towsey, " you might have heard something of the law reports of yesterday.".

" No," said Peregrine, " feeling himself burn-

ng with blushes, while his hands and feet were
icy cold,—" No."

" I hope," said Miss Grayson, " you got your
dressing-case and umbrella, safe from Slambury,
Mr. Bunce."

This did not improve Peregrine's position.
He merely stammered out something like an
acknowledgment of her attention.

" Well," said Towsey, " where are my honey-
mooners? we must get them in. Mrs. Nobbatop, luncheon time is past."

" Ah," said Mrs. Nobbatop, turning to Peregrine, not even yet alive to the brutality—for
that is the only suitable word—of his conduct,
" and *you* enjoy luncheon *so*."

" I assure you," said Peregrine, " I merely
came over just to ———"

At this moment the sound of a key bugle,
tuning up " Molly put the kettle on," or some
such classical melody, struck upon Peregrine's
ears—it was annihilation—too surely did he
recognize the sound.

" What is that music ?" said Mrs. Nobbatop.

" It is the way my friend McLarrup has of announcing his approach to the house," said Towsey, " so now we may get to our refreshment ; he and his charming wife will be here directly."

" Why," said Peregrine, getting up hastily, and gathering together his hat, gloves, and whip, " I never eat luncheon, and besides, I must get back. I only rode down to pay my respects, and ———"

Tootle tootle went the key bugle, close to the windows.

" Well, then," said Maria, rising from the sofa, with a coolness of manner which it required a powerful struggle to assume and maintain, " we will not detain you any longer. I understand that Captain and Mrs. McLarrup *were* friends of yours`. Perhaps you have no particular desire now to meet them. That desire on *your* part towards *them* is precisely equal, Sir, to *my* desire as regards *yourself*. Aunt, ring the bell for Mr. Bunce's horses."

How Mr. Peregrine Bunce, under such circumstances, effected his retreat, history does not tell; but certain it is, that as he took his final departure, the key bugle of Captain McLarrup *did* sound forth " Stole away," in a tone which, however brilliant in itself, rang most discordantly in the defeated pretender's ears. His abdication was followed by a loud laugh, of which, it is to be hoped, he was unconscious; and the cause of which, even then, the amiable, good Mrs. Nobbatop did not quite comprehend. A more signal defeat never fell upon a meaner or more despicable hero.

END OF VOL. II.

LONDON :

GILBERT AND RIVINGTON, PRINTERS,

ST. JOHN'S SQUARE.

32101 063581217

162

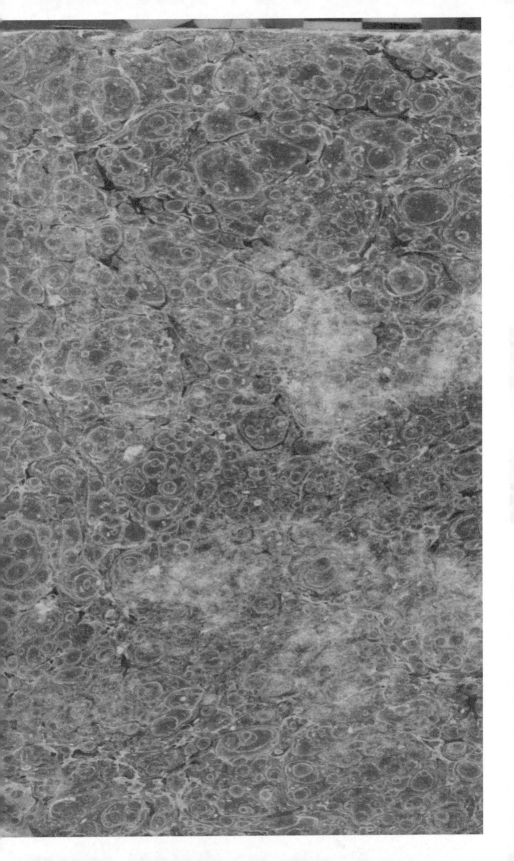

Check Out More Titles From HardPress Classics Series In this collection we are offering thousands of classic and hard to find books. This series spans a vast array of subjects – so you are bound to find something of interest to enjoy reading and learning about.

Subjects:
Architecture
Art
Biography & Autobiography
Body, Mind &Spirit
Children & Young Adult
Dramas
Education
Fiction
History
Language Arts & Disciplines
Law
Literary Collections
Music
Poetry
Psychology
Science
…and many more.

Visit us at www.hardpress.net

CPSIA information can be obtained
at www.ICGtesting.com
Printed in the USA
BVHW091904220819
556561BV00021B/4800/P

9 781406 996289